The Science of Life After Death

New Research Shows

Human Consciousness

Lives On

D1328029

The Science of Life After Death

New Research Shows Human Consciousness Lives On

by

Stephen Hawley Martin

THE OAKLEA PRESS

RICHMOND, VIRGINIA

ISBN 10: 1-892538-52-0
ISBN 13: 978-1-892538-52-9

The Oaklea Press
6912 Three Chopt Road, Suite B
Richmond, Virginia 23226

Voice: 1-800-295-4066
Facsimile: 1-804-281-5686

Web site: http://www.OakleaPress.com

Contents

Foreword

I have two primary objectives for this book.

First is to demonstrate that you are eternal. Your body may die, but your consciousness will live on. You see, you are spirit, what I will call "life force," that has come into the physical dimension for a reason. I hope this book will encourage you to find the particular reason you came here at the time and place you did.

Second, I would like this book to help establish a new world view. The western world is long overdue for such a shift. The current world view, which dates from the nineteenth century, is that the universe, the solar system and our bodies, can be compared to machines. Everything is separate, and even our bodies and our minds are assemblies of separate parts. It seems incredibly odd to me that we would have this materialistic world view at a time when physicists assure us that no such thing as solid or separate stuff exists. All is energy—vibrations. You are energy. I am energy. All is energy.

With this in mind, I respectfully request that you make an effort to suspend disbelief as you read ahead. Support for my thesis will unfold and build as the chapters roll by.

What, then, is my thesis? It is that all is one, that there is one mind from which everything in the universe, including you and me, emanates. It is that through a natural process, this one mind has become subdivided so that we each have our own unique consciousness and perspective. But, nonetheless, we remain connected to and an integral aspect of the one mind.

In addition to stating my objectives, I would also like to use this space to offer an apology. The terminology I have elected to use for what I refer to alternatively as the Universal Mind, the life force, subjective mind, Tao, and ground of being may be offensive to some and confusing to others. All these terms refer to the same thing, or perhaps more accurately, to aspects of the same thing. Perhaps, some day science will come up with a single term we can all readily understand.

Those of a religious bent may believe I should have used the word, God. In some cases I have done so. But for the most part I have avoided this term because I know it carries negative connotations for some and for others conjures up an image that would be misleading.

Stephen Hawley Martin

July, 2009

Chapter One
Consciousness Outside the Body

Pam Reynolds

Pam Reynolds was only 35 years old when she was told she was going to die.

She'd been suffering dizziness and loss of speech, so her doctor had ordered a CAT scan. Huge aneurysms—two ballooned arteries— were found at the base of her brain near where the stem entered her spine. It would only be a matter of time before one burst. When that happened, Pam's life would come to an end.

Surgery seemed out of the question. One aneurysm was in an almost impossible place to reach without injuring the brain. If the skull were opened, the brain would be in the way—between the aneurysm and the doctor's scalpel.

As good fortune would have it, one long shot possibility did exist. Dr. Robert Spetzler, chief of neurosurgery at the Barrow Neurological Institute in Phoenix, Arizona, offered a radical procedure that would require shutting down Pam's body. Her heart would be stopped. Her body temperature would be lowered to sixty degrees Fahrenheit so there would be little or no deterioration of tissue. The blood would be drained from her brain, and then—only then, because he would in effect be working on a cadaver—Dr. Spetzler could deal with the the most difficult to reach aneurysm.

Incredible as it may seem, Pam would literally be dead. If anyone

9

Barrow Neurological Institute

ever wanted to construct an experiment to find out what happens when we die, this would have been it—provided, of course, Pam actually came back from death to tell the tale.

The procedure was awfully scary, but it was her only chance, so Pam went ahead with it. With no blood running through her brain, the aneurysm would deflate, and the doctor would be able to repair it. Once repaired, the plan was for the surgical team to pump blood back into her through a device that would raise its temperature and along with it, that of her body. Then they would jolt her heart back to life using electric shocks.

Imagine how Pam must have felt when they wheeled her into the operating room on the gurney, wheels squeaking. That was at 7:15 a.m. on August 8, 1991. Anesthesia was administered, both ear channels were occluded with molded ear speakers designed to monitor brain stem function. These clicked constantly. An electroencephalogram (EEG) was set up to monitor cortical brain waves, and an electrical device was affixed to test the functioning of her cerebral hemispheres. These machines would display flat lines once her heart was stopped and her blood drained out.

Pam remembers none of this and remained unconscious until she heard a buzzing sound at 8:40 a.m.—an unpleasant sound, she recalls, reminiscent of a dentist's drill.

Recounting this she said, "I remember the top of my head tingling, and I just sort of popped out of it. Then, I was looking down at my body. I knew it was my body, but for some reason I didn't care.

"My vantage point was that of sitting on the doctor's shoulder. He had an instrument in his hand that looked like an electric toothbrush. That puzzled me. I had assumed they would open the skull with a saw—I'd heard the term 'saw'—but what he was working with looked a lot more like a drill than a saw—sort of like my electric toothbrush—and there also was a case, like the one my father stored his socket wrenches in when I was a child—with little bits in it."

All this turned out to be true. The saw used by the doctor did look like an electric toothbrush, and there was a case with bits in it. The extraordinary thing is, Pam could not have made these observations about tools as she entered the operating room because she would not have been able to see them. All the instruments, including the drill-like saw, were concealed inside sterile packaging, as is standard practice. To maintain a sterile environment, these packages are not opened until the patient is completely asleep.

"I also heard people talking," she continued. "I distinctly remember hearing a female voice say, 'We have a problem. The arteries are too small.'

"Someone said to try the other side.

"This [talking] seemed to come from somewhere down at the other end of the table and I wondered, *What are they doing? This is brain surgery [not surgery on the legs].*

"I later found out they accessed the femoral arteries, which are in the groin area, in order to drain the blood from my body."

Operation records show that the artery first accessed for this purpose could not be used because it was indeed too small, so the artery on the other side was used. Dr. Spetzler verified that no one would be able to hear or see anything, using the usual bodily senses, while in the state Pam Reynolds was in at the time.

But Pam did hear and see what was going on. Her consciousness was outside her body. But it didn't remain in the operating room as surgery progressed.

"I felt a presence, and I turned around to look at it," she said. "That's when I saw a tiny pinpoint of light.

"It [the light] started to pull me. There was a physical sensation like what you might have in your stomach when you drive fast over a hill. So I went toward the light, and as I came closer I began to discern different figures.

"I distinctly heard my grandmother call me. She had a very distinct voice, and I immediately went to her. It felt great. And I saw an uncle who had passed away when he was only 39 years old. He had taught me a lot. He taught me to play my first guitar. I saw many people I knew and many I did not know.

"I asked if God was the light, and the answer was, 'No, God is not the light. The light is what happens when God breathes.' And I remember thinking, I'm standing in the breath of God.

"At some point I was reminded that it was time to go back. Of course, I'd made my decision to go back before the operation, but the more I was there in the light, the more I liked it.

"But my uncle escorted me back down the tunnel.

"When I got to where the body was, and I looked at it, I really did not want to get in it. I was certain about that because it looked like what it was—void of life. And I knew it would hurt.

"But my uncle kept reasoning with me. He said not to worry and go ahead. It would be like diving into a swimming pool.

"'Just jump in,' he said.

"'No,' I said.

"'What about the children?'

"'You know, I think the children will be just fine.'

"'Honey, you've got to go.'

"'No.'

"I saw the body jump.

"Then he pushed me, and I felt [my body] jump.

"It took me a long time, but I guess I'm ready [now] to forgive him for that."

The jump Pam saw, and the one she felt, were caused by the electric shocks to restart her heart.

All this happened under extremely controlled conditions when every known vital sign, every clinical sign of life, and death, was being monitored. Her body had been dead, but her consciousness had lived on.

The doctors have no explanation. They know of no way to explain what Pam experienced given the paradigm science operates within at this time in history. Pam's ability to recall and accurately describe what was going on in the operating room while she was dead with the blood drained from her head and most of her body, indicates her mind had separated from her brain. But today's generally accepted scientific reasoning holds that there can be no memory of anything when the heart is stopped and the brain is not functioning. The only logical explanation is that her consciousness was outside her brain and the memories of her experiences formed there as well.

If this were an isolated case, perhaps it could be dismissed as some sort of anomaly. Certainly, skeptics would try. But there are many, many others. Once such is that reported by Dr. Melvin E. Morse, M.D.

The Case of Kristle Merzlock

In spring, 1982, Kristle Merzlock arrived at the hospital in Pocatello, Idaho, in a coma—having been pulled from the bottom of a swimming pool. Her heart had stopped beating 19 minutes earlier.

Bill Longhurst, the physician who received Kristle in the emergency room, quickly summoned Melvin Morse, then 27, the only doctor at the hospital who'd performed a significant number of resuscitations. Miraculously, he was able to get her heart going and put her on an artificial lung machine.

Melvin E. Morse, M.D.

Morse had topflight academic credentials—a medical degree with honors from George Washington University and a research fellowship funded by the National Cancer Institute. Even so, he was not prepared for what was about to happen. Kristle's pupils were fixed and dilated and she had no gag reflex. A CAT scan revealed massive swelling of her brain, an artificial lung was doing her breathing, and her blood pH was extremely acidic, a clear indication of imminent death. Morse said, "There was little we could do at that point."

But somehow, against all odds, Kristle survived. Three days later she came out of her coma with full brain function. Needless to say, Morse was amazed. But something else amazed him even more and, eventually, forced him to completely rearrange his thinking about consciousness and life after death.

Kristle recognized him.

"That's the one with the beard," she told her mother. "First there was this tall doctor who didn't have a beard, and then he came in."

This was true. Morse had a beard, and the admitting doctor, Longhurst, was clean-shaven and tall.

Kristle then described the emergency room with astonishing accuracy.

Morse said, "She had the right equipment, the right number of people—everything was just as it had been that day." She correctly related the procedures that had been performed on her. Even though her eyes had been closed and she had been profoundly comatose during the entire experience, she still 'saw' what was going on."

Kristle was able to do this, she said, because she was outside her body—that is, her mind and awareness were outside floating above it, observing what was going on. As you might expect, Morse had a hard time believing what she told him about her out-of-body experience (OBE), and his skepticism showed through. Kristle patted him shyly on the hand and said, "Don't worry, Dr. Morse, heaven is fun!"

Morse wrote up her case for the American Medical Association's *Pediatric Journal* as a "fascinoma," meaning a strange yet interesting case. Then he returned to cancer research. One night, he saw Elizabeth Kübler-Ross on television describing to a grieving mother what her child went through when she died. Kübler-Ross said that the girl floated out of her body, suffered no pain, and entered into heaven. Morse thought this was unprofessional of a psychiatrist, and vowed to prove her wrong.

NDE Research by Morse and Sharp

He teamed up with Kimberly Clark Sharp, a clinical social worker in Seattle to begin researching near-death experiences (NDEs) in children. Their work later became known as *The Seattle Study*. At Seattle Children's Hospital, they designed and implemented the first prospective study of NDEs with age and sex matched controls. They studied 26 children who nearly died and compared them to 131 children who were also quite ill, in the intensive care unit, mechanically ventilated, treated with drugs such as morphine, Valium and anesthetic agents. Often they had suffered a lack of oxygen to the brain, but none had ever reached the near-death state of actually being clinically dead.

Kimberly Clark Sharp

Before 1976, not much had been published on NDEs, but that year a medical student named Raymond Moody published what became a best-selling book called *Life After Life*. Moody interviewed patients who had been resuscitated after being clinically dead and described what he found to be common occurrences in such instances: a sensation of serenity, separation from the body, entrance into a dark tunnel, a vision of light, and the appearance of deceased family members who offer help.

Morse said working with kids had its advantages. "The adult near-death experience is cluttered by cultural references and contaminated by the need for validation," he explained. "But with kids, it's pure. Kids don't repress the memory, or fear the ridicule that might come from talking about it."

He found that of the 26 children who nearly died 23 had NDEs whereas none of the other children had them. If NDEs are caused by a lack of oxygen to the brain, drugs, hallucinations secondary to coma, or stress and the fear of dying, then the control would have been expected to also have had NDEs, but they did not, indicating that NDEs happen only to the dying.

Morse was determined, he said, to "produce a study that would hold up under the most stringent peer review." He poured over the medical records of each patient, documenting the drugs they took, the anesthesia used on them and the level of oxygen in their blood. His team of medical students combed the literature in search of reports of drug use, psychological states or oxygen deprivation that might have produced hallucinations similar to near-death experiences.

When he published his results in the *American Journal of Diseases of Children,* Morse felt he was on solid ground in asserting near-death experiences are not the result of drugs or sleep deprivation, nor are they merely dreams or hallucinations. He was extremely careful to stay on firm scientific ground, labeling them "natural psychological processes associated with dying." While he could not explain what caused NDEs, he could prove that something consistent was going on, something that could not be explained in medical terms.

If you think Morse's colleagues and the medical community toasted him, and gave him a pat on the back, you are wrong. Morse was ridiculed and scorned by other doctors. Soon, prominent physicians questioned whether he could even deliver good patient care.

What I call "pseudo skeptics" have advanced a number of theories to explain the visions of dying patients. I call them pseudo skeptics because they will come up with almost ridiculous ways to attempt to shoot down what is clearly obvious based on solid data. Some attributed the NDEs to "anesthetic agents" administered in the hospital, even though Morse found that many of the subjects studied were dying far from a hospital setting. Others considered the visions to be hallucinations produced by narcotics, endorphins or profound oxygen deprivation—none of which, Morse insists, have been shown to correlate with the near death experiences he documented. He believes the medical community rejected his conclusions for a variety of reasons—one being his willingness to talk about death as a positive experience.

He said, "There's a feeling that people come to doctors to keep living, that if death is treated as a result that isn't necessarily negative, then we may not do all we can to avoid it."[*]

This does not ring true to me. I believe a small percentage of scientists with a vested interest in maintaining the status quo have intimidated the majority into holding on the the old paradigm that says consciousness cannot exist outside the brain. We will soon look at studies that clearly show that consciousness can exist outside the brain. For now, let's look what is typically reported to happen during a near death experience.

---

[*] Several sources were consulted in putting together this anecdote including an article entitled "Spirited Away" appearing in the February 2006 issue of *Reader's Digest.*

The Elements of Near Death Experiences

In December, 2008, I interviewed consciousness researcher Jody Long, who along with her husband, Jeffrey P. Long, M.D., founded the Near Death Experience Research Foundation. They maintain what they believe is the largest NDE web site (www.nderf.org) in the world. It has more than 1800 full-text published NDE accounts.

Five steps seem to be common to NDEs:

- A sense of being dead, including the sudden awareness of a fatal accident, or of not surviving an operation.
- An out-of-body experience; the sensation of peering down on one's body. As in the cases recounted above, those experiencing clinical death often report back the scene with uncanny accuracy, quoting doctors and witnesses verbatim.
- Some kind of tunnel experience, a sense of moving upward or through a narrow passage.
- Light, including light "beings," God or a Godlike entity. For those having a hell-like experience, the opposite may be true—darkness or a lack of light.
- A life review—being shown one's life, sometimes highlighting one's mistakes or omissions.

I find the life review of particular significance, and it never fails to come to mind whenever I'm tempted to do something that potentially might harm another. Here is what Raymond Moody, M.D., author of *Life After Life* and other books on this subject had to say about the life review:

Raymond Moody, M.D.

When the life review occurs, there are no more physical surroundings. In their place is a full color, three-dimensional, panoramic review of every single thing the [persons having this experience] have done in their lives.

This usually takes place in a third-person perspective and doesn't occur in time as we know it. The closest description I've heard of it is that the person's whole life is there at once.

In this situation, you not only see every action that you have ever done, but you also perceive immediately the effect of every single one of your actions upon the people in your life.

So for instance, if I see myself doing an unloving act, then immediately I am in the consciousness of the person I did that act to, so that I feel their sadness, hurt, and regret.

On the other hand, if I do a loving act to someone, then I am immediately in their place and I can feel the kind and happy feelings.

Through all of this, the Being is with those people, asking them what good they have done with their lives. He helps them through this review and helps them put all the events of their life in perspective.

All of the people who go through this come away believing that the most important thing in their life is love.

For most of them, the second most important thing in life is knowledge. As they see life scenes in which they are learning things, the Being points out that one of the things they can take with them at death is knowledge. The other is love.

Chapter Two
Awareness Is Non Local

Rhine Research Center

Back in the early 1930s a university with a new name and big ambitions hired a couple of men who wanted to unravel the mysteries of the paranormal. That university was Duke, located in Durham, North Carolina, now one of the most prestigious in the United States. The men were William McDougall and Joseph Banks Rhine, most often referred to as J. B. Rhine. The organization they created was called the Duke Parapsychology Laboratory for many years. Today it is called The Rhine Research Center, and although it is no longer connected with the University, it is located adjacent to the Duke campus.

What motivated these men? They wanted most to prove or disprove the fact or fiction of life after death. On my radio show that aired the week of April 6, 2009, I interviewed journalist Stacy Horn who wrote a book chronicling the history of this organization from 1930 to 1960, including experiments that were conducted and the interaction of the many people over the years. This included such well-known celebrities Upton Sinclair and scientists such as Albert Einstein. The name of her book is *UNBE-*

Stacy Horn

LIEVABLE: Investigations into Ghosts, Poltergeists, Telepathy, and Other Unseen Phenomena, from the Duke Parapsychology Laboratory (HarperCollins, ECCO Imprint, 2009). Stacy went into this project a skeptic about paranormal phenomena, but was no longer a skeptic when she came out of it.

Previously known as Trinity College, a grant by tobacco millionaire James B. Duke in 1924 prompted the name change. Perhaps, the newly reconstituted school was looking for ways to make its mark when it lured William McDougall from Harvard University to set up a department of psychology.

He was soon contacted by a man named John Thomas who had 800 pages of transcripts generated by mediums he had been working with. Thomas' wife had died unexpectedly during an operation, and Thomas had been devastated. He began working with mediums in order to communicate with her.

Thomas got exciting results, but he wasn't sure he could believe them. Looking for verification of their authenticity, he traveled around the United States talking with mediums. He went to Europe, eventually, reasoning that mediums there would have no way of knowing anything about him or his wife. If they were able to come up with information that was accurate, it would be more convincing.

Ultimately, Thomas wrote to McDougall asking if he could send J. B. Rhine, then of Harvard University, and Rhine's wife Louisa, to Duke to study this material. McDougall agreed and Rhine came to Duke.

J. B. Rhine Takes Up Residence at Duke

J. B. Rhine (1895-1980)

Rhine studied Thomas' transcripts. He was able to verify much of the information, and to all but eliminate fraud and lucky guesses. He traveled to Upstate New York, for example, investigating cemetery head stones to check out the veracity of genealogy of Thomas' wife indicated by a medium. The genealogy proved to be accurate. Not even Thomas himself knew if this genealogy was correct, but the information did check out. Ultimately, however, Rhine concluded that even though the information was correct, it could not be said with absolute certainty that the information was coming from Thomas' deceased, and now disembodied, wife.

The problem still dogs researchers who study the purported abilities of mediums. Assuming no fraud is being perpetrated, several possibilities exist as to the source of information coming from mediums that seems to be from a deceased individual:

1. It may actually be coming from the now disembodied individual.

2. The medium may be employing ESP or telepathy to read the minds of living individuals—in this case Thomas himself, or other living relatives of his wife. Indeed, a whole range of psychic abilities may be put to use including remote viewing, psychometry and clairvoyance. Nowadays, the full breadth of psychic abilities that might be at work is called "superpsi."

3. A third possibility is that the medium might be tapping into a reservoir of information of human history, thoughts and feelings many believe exists. Some call this the Akashic Records, which are envisioned as the memory hard drive of the universe. The famous psychiatrist, Carl Jung, for example, wrote of a universal unconscious that holds the history and thoughts of all mankind. Today, researchers call this the "psychic reservoir." This is thought to be the source of information for perhaps most famous and well-documented psychic of the twentieth century, Edgar Cayce (1877-1945), often referred to as "The Sleeping Prophet"— Cayce became known as such because his readings were given while in a self-induced trance.

Rhine could find no way to prove superpsi, or the psychic reservoir, were not the source of information tapped into by mediums who had supposedly been in touch with Thomas' wife. So Rhine began putting his energy into the study of what became known as extra sensory perception, or ESP. He reasoned that if he could prove awareness extends beyond, and exists outside the body, a major step would be taken toward establishing the possibility of survival of consciousness after death. After all, for our consciousness to continue after death it has to be capable of existing outside the body and the brain. This chapter will establish this.

Conclusive Proof ESP

Rhine's most famous experiment used what has become known as ESP cards. Developed specifically for this purpose, these had different symbols on them including a star, wavy lines, a cross, a box and a circle. Many of these experiments were conducted—

ESP Cards

mostly using Duke University students—to see if people could tell what symbols were on the cards without looking at them. It was found again and again that they could.

The controls employed in these experiments were refined over time until neither the students nor those testing them could see one another. Ultimately, research was conducted in such a way that not even the person conducting the experiment knew what symbol was on the card a student was to identify. The experiments turned up statistically significant results time after time, showing without a doubt ESP is real. This, by the way, supports my one-mind theory stated in the Foreword.

One of Rhine's subjects in the ESP experiments was particularly impressive. A divinity student, his name was Hubert Pierce. Rhine believed that everyone possessed psychic abilities, but his research indicates some people have more talent for it than others. This is of course true of other abilities. An extremely talented singer will wow the judges and go on to win American Idol, but most will fail miserably and get the boot at the first audition.

There were twenty-five cards in the ESP deck, and five different symbols. Therefore, one would expect to guess five correctly each time through, simply by chance. Hubert Pierce could consistently get more than five correct, as could a number of others. But the interesting thing is, and according to Stacy Horn this came up frequently in the research, emotions played a role. Hubert, for example, needed money. He was a poor, struggling college student. Rhine once told him if he got the next card right, he'd pay him a hundred dollars. Pierce got it right. Rhine said, "Okay, get the next one right, and you'll get another hundred dollars."

Pierce got the next one right.

This went on through the entire deck. Pierce named all 25 cards correctly.

At one point, however, Hubert said he would not be coming into the lab for tests. His girlfriend had broken up with him, and he was heartbroken.

When he finally did come back, he did not perform well.

Another example of emotions playing a roll was the time Rhine tested the psychic abilities of children at a orphanage. One little girl became quite attached to a woman researcher. The little girl performed extremely well, apparently because she was eager to please, and wanted to prolong the session.

The Phenomenon of Remote Viewing

Something that demonstrates awareness is not local, but rather is non local—at no particular place but everywhere at once—is the phenomenon of remote viewing. Those adept at remote viewing can direct their consciousness to be any where they want it to be.

Remote viewers use psychic powers to observe what's happening at a location some distance from them—in terms both of miles and in some cases, time as well.

Back in the 1970s, the U. S. government learned that the KGB was using psychics to spy on the United States. Naturally, U.S. Intelligence leaders wanted to see if this actually worked.

Did it? U.S. Army Major General Edmund R. Thompson, who was deputy Director for the Management and Operations for Defense Intelligence from 1982-84 is quoted as having said, "I never liked to get into debates with the skeptics, because if you didn't believe that remote viewing was real, you hadn't done your homework."

Remote viewing was used from the early 1970s forward through the Cold War to keep tabs on what the Soviets and Eastern Block countries were up to that couldn't be observed by spy planes, or satellites, or operatives on the ground.

In the Spring of 2009, I interviewed F. Holmes Atwater, the man who in 1979 set up the U.S. Army Intelligence unit responsible called Stargate. His friends know him by the name of Skip.

The Story of F. Holmes Atwater

Skip Atwater

Skip got into this line of work through a series of what some people might call amazing coincidences, and others would say are syncronicities—events that look like coincidences, but seem to happen for a reason.

Skip grew up in a home with parents that took such things for granted. It was the sort of thing they talked about at the dinner table. As a kid, Skip would go off on out-of-body trips almost nightly. He related one specific story to me and my listeners to illustrate this. He was seven or eight years old at the time, and it had to do with a problem he had with bedwetting.

"It was embarrassing," he said. "I had a big, brown piece of rubber on my bed so I wouldn't ruin the mattress. My parents didn't scold me, but they did make me responsible for washing my own sheets.

"I can remember distinctly waking up one night, and I was all wet. I was screaming in anger, and my mother came in and said, 'What's wrong? Did you fall out of bed?'

"I said, 'No, I remember, I got up, and I went down the hall to the bathroom, and I sat down. And the minute I started to pee, I woke up here in bed, and I'm all wet.'

"I was mad as the dickens, and my mother hugged me and said, 'Oh, that's all right, don't worry about it. You know, Skip, sometimes you're in your body and sometimes you're out of your body, and you have to remember that when you're going to the bathroom, make sure you're in your body.'

"[What she said] made perfect sense to me, and I said, 'Oh, now I understand,' and that was the end of my bedwetting."

Atwater Learns of Remote Viewing

Skip was in Army working for Army Intelligence when he came across a book called *Mind Reach* by Russell Targ and Harold E. Puthoff of the Stanford Research Institute. The book explained remote viewing, which didn't seem at all unusual to Skip given his experiences as a child. Naturally, a person could see things at a distance, using his mental powers. It was as though a light had suddenly flicked on. He instantly realized this could be used to gather intelligence.

At the time, Skip was in counter intelligence. It was his job to defend against wiretaps, bugging devices, and other forms of intelligence gathering by the enemy. No one in his counter intelligence unit had thought about remote viewing as a way the enemy might be spying on us. So Skip went to his commanding officer, a Colonel Webb, and gave him the book. After the Colonel had read it, Skip asked him if this remote viewing was being used on our side.

The Colonel had no idea. He thought if anything was going on, the Pentagon would be the place to find out. So he had Skip transferred to the Pentagon to take a position where he'd be in charge of a counter intelligence team. Skip would have the access he needed to find out about remote viewing and what if anything was being done about it to prevent the enemy from using it.

Before Skip was able to relocate to Washington, however, he received a change of orders. He was told to report to Fort Meade in Maryland. This was a better location for a young Army officer with a wife and children, which Skip had, because Fort Meade had family housing and good schools. It would be a much more affordable and pleasant place to live than Washington, D.C.

Documents Reveal U. S. Interest in Remote Viewing

At Fort Meade, Skip was assigned to what was known as a SAVE team—Security Activity Vulnerability Estimate team. The job was to go to sensitive U.S. installations and try to penetrate them in any way possible—as the enemy might in order to gather intelligence. Then the team would make a report to the commanding officer and provide recommendations for improving security.

Skip moved into his new job and was assigned an office that had just been vacated. The file cabinet and most of the desk drawers had been cleaned out, and an office safe had been emptied, but he did come across three documents in a bottom drawer of the desk that turned out to be classified. They reported on remote viewing experiments taking place in the Soviet sphere, funded by the KGB.

Skip took the documents to his supervising officer, a Major Keenan.

The Major looked at them. "Oh, yes, I remember these," he said. "The Lt. Colonel was very interested in this subject. Do you know anything about it?"

"Why, yes, I do, Major."

The Major took a moment and sized up Skip. "Lieutenant," he said, "from now on you're in charge of it."

And that's how in Skip got his wish and started on a ten year career that eventually put him in charge of a remote viewing unit of the Army.

Atwater Learns about Remote Viewing

Skip soon learned that basic research had been underway since 1972 to check the validity of the Eastern Block experiments. The initial question had been whether reports of success were valid. It might be the Soviets were falsifying the results to create fear. The Stanford Research Institute had been retained to replicate the experiments paid for by the KGB. To the surprise of our intelligence community, the results had been positive.

By the time Skip got involved, the CIA and other U.S. intelligence agencies had been using natural psychics for some time to gather information, including well-known psychics such as Ingo Swann, who has since written several books on remote viewing. Skip's job became to set up, recruit and train remote viewers for U.S. Army Intelligence who may or not have had prior experience using psychic abilities. He developed a screening process, and for those who made the cut, a training program employing methodologies gleaned from accomplished remote viewers.

Skip's efforts met with success, but after a while he began looking for ways to enhance the results his remote viewers were achieving. This led him to The Monroe Institute (TMI) in Virginia, where he now works as Research Director.

The Monroe Institute Proves to Be a Resource

Robert Monroe (1915–1995) had spent a career in broadcasting, culminating as a vice president of NBC Radio. After leaving NBC, Monroe became known for his research into altered states of consciousness. His 1971 book *Journeys Out of the Body* is said to have popularized the term "out-of-body experience," or OBE.

Robert Monroe

Monroe's original objective had been to develop a process by which people could learn effortlessly—while they were asleep. He developed sound patterns that would help people reach a state called Stage Two Sleep and hold them in that state. Monroe experimented on himself and exposed himself to many varieties of sound. One night in 1956, quite unexpectedly, he found himself floating over his body. He panicked and thought the must be dying. He consulted medical doctors and psychiatrists about this, and eventually under-

The Monroe Institute

stood he wasn't dying—that this experience was fairly common. As a result, he conducted more experiments to learn how to replicate what he had done, and to control it.

By the time Monroe came to Skip's attention, he had established The Monroe Institute southwest of Charlottesville, Virginia, where the public could come to share in these sound-created experiences. Skip decided to investigate, and traveled from Fort Meade to Virginia meet Monroe.

Skip, of course, was running a secret program for the U.S. Army and could not disclose the real reason for his visit. But he did explain to Monroe that he was interested in the work being done, had read his book, and had had out-of-body experiences as a child.

Monroe invited Skip to come into his laboratory. He took him to a room that had been set up and equipped for his experiments. He had Skip lie down. Skip became nervous. He was, after all, an intelligence officer on a surreptitious mission.

"What are these sounds I've heard about—these hemi-sync® sounds?" Skip asked.

"Oh, nothing to worry about," Monroe said. "I'll just play some music at first to calm you down."

As soon as Skip was lying down on the bed with the head phones on, the door shut and the lights went out. He wondered what he'd gotten himself into.

Music came through the speakers. It turned into the sound of surf against the shore. This reminded Skip of happy childhood days spent playing at the beach.

Then droning sounds came on in the background and quite unexpectedly the bed began to rise off the floor as though it were being lifted by hydraulics the way a car in a service station is lifted for an oil change.

Skip thought, *Wow, this is a very special bed. They must have one of those lifts underneath it to push it up in the air.*

As he was thinking about what must have been done to build it—the building had to have been constructed around it—he began to feel himself moving in a different direction. He seemed to be headed laterally, rather than up. That's when he realized it must not be a lift he was on. Yet the feeling was very strong, quite visceral, as though he were on an airplane circling into a landing approach. He saw or imagined that he was moving through a rock or crystal tunnel of some kind. Then he heard a voice.

"Whoa, there. What's happening, kid?" It was Robert Monroe.

"Well, I seem to be going some place," Skip said.

"Well, now, where're you going, kid?"

"I don't know," Skip answered.

Skip traveled along the tunnel, or corridor, and eventually came out of it in vast, open, white space. He said it was a little like being in a white cloud except there was no mist or fog. Everything was white, boundless, and there were no walls.

Perhaps the strangest part was that Skip watched himself arrive.

He thought, *Gosh, I've come all this way only to find I'm already here.*

Skip said in our interview, "It sounds trite to say wherever you go, there you are, but that's exactly what happened to me."

He remained in the white space for a while. Then he heard Robert Monroe's voice again:

"What's happening?"

Skip was embarrassed because he'd forgotten he was in Monroe's laboratory lying on a bed.

He said, "Oh, nothing much."

"Okay . . . well, it's time for lunch."

This didn't make sense, but that didn't matter because Monroe changed the sounds coming through the headphones, and Skip felt the bed being lowered down to its original position. In a short time, the door was open and the lights were on.

Monroe was standing in the doorway.

Skip leaned over and looked under the bed.

"Oh, did you lose your wallet down there?" Monroe asked.

Skip was looking for the hydraulic lift, but there was none.

As a result of this experience, he learned there was definitely something to the sound technology Robert Monroe had developed, and the Army entered into a classified contract with Robert Monroe to do some training.

The Amazing Abilities of Joe McMoneagle

One man Monroe trained was perhaps the most outstanding remote viewer in the Army. His named is Joe McMoneagle.

Joe had been in intelligence before joining Skip's unit. His personal story is fascinating and was related to me by a guest on my show who'd gotten to know Joe over the years through an association with The Monroe Institute.

Joe McMoneagle

In the early 1970s, Joe was the target of a successful assassination attempt while in the Army stationed in Germany, working as an operative in intelligence. Poison was the method. He was meeting with an intelligence contact at a restaurant, having dinner, when he felt nauseous. He excused himself and went outside to get some air. He walked around for a moment, then saw a crowd gathered just outside the door. He went to see what the commotion was about, looked through the crowd, and could make out a body lying on the street.

People were saying, "He's dead, he's dead!"

Joe came closer and was shocked to see the body was his own.

Testing later showed he'd been subjected to a binary poison, one which becomes toxic when combined with another substance. This had allowed his assassin to slip him the the poison and make his getaway before Joe sat down to dinner and consumed whatever had triggered the toxicity that killed him.

McMoneagle's consciousness, after viewing his body lying on the street, went toward the light and through the tunnel described by Pam Reynolds and other near-death survivors. As is now considered typical in these cases, he arrived at a place where he was met by spiritual beings. There, he underwent some instruction and a life review.

We would know nothing of this if Joe's body had not been resuscitated. His recovery and recuperation took quite some time.

What happened that evening changed Joe in several ways. He'd had psychic experiences before his NDE, but had kept them to himself. He no longer did. He also began to have spontaneous out-of-body experiences he was unable to control.

Joe's case came to the attention of two physicists at the Stanford Research Institute, Russell Targ and Harold Puthoff. They'd already been working on a government contract to study the ramifications of the quantum mechanics theory of non locality of consciousness. These were the same experiments described in the classified document found by Skip Atwater, and the same two men who'd authored the book he'd read.

Joe became the first remote viewer directly on the government payroll. In the course of his career in the Army as a remote viewer, Joe worked on more than 200 missions, many of which were reported at the highest levels of the U.S. military and government. Some of the information was considered so crucial, vital and unavailable from any other source, that he was awarded the Legion of Merit for his work, the second highest award the Army can give to someone in the military during peacetime.

Skylab's Fall to Earth Is Accurately Predicted

One such mission was to determine the time and the location Sky-lab would fall to earth. Depending on how old you are, you may recall Skylab—literally a scientific laboratory in orbit around the earth, put there for astronauts to conduct experiments in space. Launched in 1973, it weighed about 100 tons.

Skylab

By 1979 its orbit was decaying and Skylab was expected to come down. The question was, "Where?"

A hundred ton metal object falling on a heavily populated area such as New York, Tokyo or London, for example, would cause a tremendous death and destruction. Super computers were enlisted to answer the question, but too many variables existed for the technology of the day. The results were unreliable.

Joe McMoneagle, Ingo Swann and a third individual, a woman whose name I have been unable to uncover, were contracted with individually to come up with an answer. None of the three knew the others were involved. All picked the same day, July 11, 1979, and almost the same time. Each was within five minutes of the other two. This was nine and a half months before Skylab came down. In addition, they all picked a location in western Australia within five miles of one another—a remote, uninhabited area.

Skylab came down there, all right, almost precisely as predicted, demonstrating awareness is not located just inside our skulls, nor is it limited in time and space—more evidence my one-mind theory is correct.

The Capture of Saddam Hussein Is Seen Six Weeks Ahead

Stephan Schwartz

Another startling example that awareness is non local comes from a book by Stephan A. Schwartz, *OPENING TO THE INFINITE: The Art and Science of Nonlocal Awareness* (Nemoseen Media, 2007). Mr. Schwartz was on my radio show in the summer of 2008. One of the amazing stories he told was about the predictions made by a college seminar class about the capture of Saddam Hussein. On November 2, 2003, after being taught the basic skills of remote viewing, 47 of those who'd attended the seminar agreed to "Describe the location of Saddam Hussein at the time of this capture or discovery by U.S. or coalition forces." The students' data was collected and analyzed, including points of consensus concerning the physical location, as well as things that were not likely to be predictable—such as Hussein's appearance on the day of his capture. The data were photocopied and distributed to a number of people, and then turned over to a third party, Herk Stokeley, Director of Atlantic University. Stokeley placed the data in an envelope, which he sealed in front of a notary, who affixed her seal across the envelope's flap. The envelope was then placed in a vault.

Hussein was captured about six weeks later, on December 13, 2003. The remote viewing documents in the safe said he would be beneath an ordinary looking house on the outskirts of a small village near the city of Tikrit, and that the house would be part of a small compound that's bordered on one side by a dirt road and, on the other by a nearby river. Two large palm trees would mark the ends of the house. All this turned out to be true.

Remote viewing also predicted Hussein would be found crouching in a subterranean room or cave reached by a tunnel. This was true.

Saddam at Capture

Remote viewing said Hussein would look like a homeless person with dirty rough clothing, long ratty hair and a substantial and equally ratty salt and pepper beard. This was true.

Remote viewing said he would have only two or three supporters with him at the time of his discovery. He had two.

Remote viewing said he'd have a gun with him. He had a pistol.

Remote viewing said he would have a quantity of money. He had $750,000 in cash.

Remote viewing said he would be defiant, but would not put up any resistance and would be tired and dispirited. This was true.

What's the take-away from all this? The one mind we all share contains all—past, present and future.

All truth passes through three stages:

First it is ridiculed.

Second, it is violently opposed.

Third, it is accepted as self-evident.

Arthur Schopenhauer

(1788 – 1860)

Chapter Three
Proof of Accurate Information
about the Dead

One young scientist has proven beyond the shadow of a doubt it's possible for bona fide mediums to relate accurate and specific information about deceased individuals to living loved ones under blinded conditions—without the use fraud, visual or verbal clues, or any other possible deceit or deception. Her name is Julie Beischel, and she has a Ph.D. in pharma-

Julie Beischel, Ph.D.

cology and toxicology. This may be an unusual background for a paranormal researcher, but it may also be the reason she has been able to come up with an airtight methodology that proves mediums can do what they have long claimed to be able to do. A big part of what pharmacologists do is determine the efficacy, or lack there of, of drugs. Doing so requires constructing foolproof, double-blind experiments.

I met with Dr. Beischel during a lunch break at the Society for Scientific Exploration's Annual Meeting in May, 2009, at the University of Virginia in Charlottesville. We talked for more than an hour. A few weeks later she also was a guest on my radio show, and I was able to ask follow up questions.

Dr. Beischel received her Ph.D. from the University of Arizona at a time something occurred to prompt her to change her career direction.

Her mother committed suicide.

The Author's Wish to Communicate with His Father

Out of a sense of propriety, I did not ask Dr. Beischel how she felt about her mother's suicide, and what questions it may have raised, but I can imagine how I would have felt had it happened in my family. The suicide of a parent must certainly be one of the most devastating events that can occur. I can imagine this because my father died when I was seven years old. He didn't commit suicide—he died of a heart attack. Nevertheless, I went through much of my life—well into adulthood—wondering if I had been the cause. The day before the night he died he'd become very angry with me. Looking back, I don't recall specifically what I did to set him off. Perhaps, I'd made a big mess in the kitchen, or written on a wall with pen or pencil. I must have done something children do to create a mess an adult has to clean up. Whatever it may have been, I can still recall how red in the face he became.

That was the last time I saw him, alive.

I assumed I'd been responsible for bringing on the heart attack that killed him. Now, with four kids of my own who have created their share of messes over the years, I can rationalize that idea away.

His life style did him in. He ate too much, and he smoked. He never exercised and he had grown a potbelly in just a couple of years. Maybe he had an unconscious death wish—who knows? Whatever the case, I now see he was a heart attack waiting to happen. But, at the age of seven, I wasn't worldly wise enough to figure that out. Suffice it to say, the question haunted me for years, "Had I caused my father's death?"

Now, think about this. Suppose I'd been able to ask a medium and get an answer—an answer I could be confident was true? Imagine how much worry and anxiety that would have saved me.

Know what? Now, thanks to Dr. Beischel, others in such a situation can do just that.

I don't know what questions Dr. Beischel may have had for her mother, but she must have had some. A basic one likely was, "Does my mother's consciousness still exist?"

Dr. Beischel told me science is her religion. Quite naturally, that's where she turned for the answer.

She wanted to know what science could tell her about life after death. "Very little," was the answer.

As fate would have it, a good deal of what little research was being done on this subject was being conducted by Dr. Gary Schwartz at the University of Arizona—precisely where Dr. beischel happened to be at the time.

From Pharmacology to Consciousness Research

A book by Schwartz detailing his work with mediums was published in 2002 by Atria Books called, *THE AFTERLIFE EXPERIMENTS: Breakthrough Scientific Evidence of Life After Death.* I understand Dr. Schwartz has been subjected to a good deal of criticism from skeptics about this research. They claim his methodologies were riddled with holes. Finding a spot for Dr. beischel in his research laboratory no doubt made a lot of sense because she was trained to come up with methodologies no one could poke holes in. For the next couple of years she worked closely with him.

When I spoke with Dr. Beischel, I asked about Dr. Schwartz's work that turned out to have been done before she joined him. She couldn't talk about that, of course, except to say when she came on board she felt more stringent controls were needed. In 2007 when Schwartz's research turned in a different direction, Dr. beischel and her husband, Mark Boccuzzi—who'd been researching hauntings—founded the Windbridge Institute for Applied Research in Human Potential.

Windbridge seems to have captured almost instant credibility in the paranormal research field. The Advisory Board reads like a who's who of respected paranormal researchers. It includes a couple whose work is reported upon in this book—Jim B. Tucker, M.D., of the University of Virginia who is researching children's memories of past lives, and Stephen Braude, Ph.D., of the University of Maryland Baltimore County who as been researching the paranormal for more than 30 years, and has written a number of books on the subject.

Airtight Methodology Is Developed

Dr. Beischel developed a methodology no one can question to test the abilities of mediums who claim to communicate with the dead. The screening process she developed takes about a year to complete. Those who pass it are certified by Windbridge, and their contact information is given on www.windbridge.com. So, if you have questions for a deceased loved one—as I did way back when—you now have a place you can go that you can feel good about.

Each prospective Windbridge medium is screened using an intensive eight-step screening and training procedure:

Step 1: Written Questionnaire

Step 2: Personality/Psychological Tests

Step 3: Phone Interview (with an existing WCRM)

Step 4: Phone Interview (with a Windbridge Investigator)

Step 5: Two Blinded Phone Readings

Step 6: Mediumship Research Training

Step 7: Human Research Subjects Training

Step 8: Grief Training

Upon successful completion of the eight steps, the medium becomes a Level One Windbridge Certified Research Medium (WCRM-1). The mediums' certification levels increase over time, from Level 1 to Level 5, as they participate in additional research studies.

Each WCRM agrees to donate a minimum of four hours per month to assist in various aspects of the research, to uphold a code of spiritual ethics, to embrace a strong commitment to the values of scientific mediumship research, and to abide by specific Windbridge standards of conduct.

Before we discuss Dr. Beischel's mediumship research, let me define some terms. A "discarnate" is a dead person with whom the medium supposedly communicates. A "sitter" is the loved one of the discarnate for whom the reading is done. A "proxy sitter" is someone who asks the questions in place of the sitter, and knows nothing about the discarnate.

The procedure is as follows. Two different, unrelated individuals are selected who would like to contact deceased loved ones. Questions are developed for the discarnates. These include such specifics as a physical description, cause of death, and the discarnate's hobbies during life. The discarnates involved must be the same sex but have different physical descriptions, occupations in life, ages and manners of death. No confusion should be possible if medium's answers are correct.

Dates and times are set for the readings, usually on separate days.

Sitters aren't told the times or dates of readings but are asked to request that the deceased loved one communicate with the right medium at the right time.

A proxy sitter who has no knowledge of the discarnates except for their first names, contacts the medium by telephone on the prescribed date and time for each reading.

Let's say the discarnates' are Suzie and Betty. The session asking the medium questions for Suzie is recorded and, later, transcribed.

On the day and time of the next reading, the questions for Betty are asked. This session is also recorded and transcribed.

In both cases, ambiguous answers are adjusted so that they lack ambiguity. For example, if the medium says Suzie's hair color was reddish, the answer is changed to "red."

Following these sessions, both sitters are given both sets of answers—without names on them. They are asked to score each item for accuracy and then rate the reports over on a scale of one to six based on how strongly they portray the loved one who was to be contacted.

This procedure eliminates the possibility of fraud. All the proxy sitter and medium have is a first name, making it impossible to find out anything about the person through conventional means. The medium cannot give answers based on visual or verbal clues because a proxy sitter who knows nothing about the discarnate asks the questions. In addition, the session is conducted by telephone.

Rater bias is also eliminated. The sitter does not know which answer sheet is for his or her loved one, and which is not.

The argument is eliminated that the answers are too general or are being judged as accurate based on wishful thinking on part of sitter because the answers deal in specifics—physical description, occupation, manner of death and so forth.

Dr. Beischel told me that discarnates often find ingenious ways to communicate their presence and survival to a loved one. In one example, the discarnate communicated to the medium about a white car the medium herself had purchased on Halloween and nicknamed "Casper"—for the friendly cartoon ghost. When asked why the discarnate might have done so, the sitter said, "Well, I suppose it's because our last name is Kasperi."

Statistically Significant Results

The results of this research have been highly significant, statistically. On a scale of one to six—with one being not at all accurate, and six extremely accurate—the average score is about 3.5 for readings containing the loved one's answers, and less than 2.0 for the control readings. That's a sizable difference.

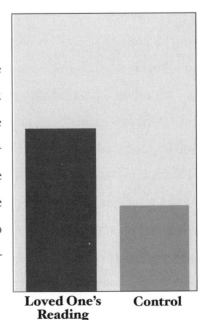

Loved One's Reading   **Control**

The scores just stated are of compilations of many readings averaged together. Some scores are considerably higher and some lower, including low scores in which the discarnate may have decided not to participate. PDFs of peer reviewed papers giving all the details can be downloaded for review by anyone interested at the Windbridge web site, www.Windbridge.org.

Dr. Beischel told me that after a research session is done, sitters often contact the mediums directly for a follow up session. Follow up sessions normally produce accuracy scores in the neighborhood of 85 to 90 percent.

The most obvious explanation for the findings of this research is that human consciousness continues after death. This is supported by research being conducted at the University of Virginia by Jim B. Tucker, M.D., that will be covered later, and by the Pam Reynolds and Kristle Merzlock near death case histories recounted in Chapter One. It is also supported by the experiences of the mediums themselves. All consistently report a difference between a session communicating with a discarnate, and what is called a psychic reading, which is done for a living person. They typically feel a presence when dealing with a discarnate.

CONTEMPORARY METHODS USED IN
LABORATORY-BASED MEDIUMSHIP RESEARCH[1]

By Julie Beischel

ABSTRACT: As with the study of any natural phenomenon, bringing mediumship into the regulated environment of the laboratory allows for the controlled and repeated examination of anomalous information reception by mediums. It also lends statistically analyzed evidence regarding the survival of consciousness hypothesis and addresses the relationship between consciousness and brain. Ideally, laboratory-based mediumship research includes 2 equally important factors: (a) a research environment that optimizes the mediumship process for both the medium and the hypothesized discarnate and (b) research methods that maximize the experimental blinding of the medium, the rater, and the experimenter in order to eliminate all conventional explanations for the information and its accuracy and specificity. The Windbridge Institute for Applied Research in Human Potential utilizes several methods that build upon historical as well as modern mediumship investigations in order to meet these 2 research goals. The research methods discussed include: detailed research reading protocols; the pairing and formatting of readings; experimental blinding; the thorough screening of all research participants; and a specific scoring system used by raters.

The analysis of information conveyed by mediums (individuals who report experiencing regular communication with the deceased) is important for several reasons:

- The survival of consciousness (i.e., the continued existence, separate from the body, of an individual's consciousness, personality, identity, or self after physical death) is a vital issue to many people. The general public's deep concern with survival and mediumship is illustrated by the recent rise of these topics in popular television shows, books, and movies.
- Investigating the phenomenon of anomalous information reception (AIR) by mediums is essential in understanding the mind's perception and processing of nonlocal, nonsensory information.
- An extensive understanding of the information mediums report and the process by which they report it is necessary in order for such information to be sensibly utilized by society. For example, mediums may be able to regularly and consistently find missing persons and contribute to criminal investigations if parameters such as error rates can be identified. Furthermore, because the source of the information anomalously reported by mediums has

[1] An earlier version of this paper was presented by the author at the Rhine Research Center conference "Consciousness Today," Myrtle Beach, South Carolina, March 23-25, 2007.

**This Peer Reviewed Paper Can
Be Downloaded at
www.Windbridge.org**

How You Can Contact a Deceased Loved One

If you are wondering about a deceased loved one or have questions you'd like him or her to answer, you might consider having a reading done. Simply go to the Windbridge.org home page and click on "Meet the Mediums." You'll find an alphabetical listing of certified mediums along with their contact information.

Dr. Beischel says one will jump out at you.

She also says the best way to have the reading done is over the phone. This way the medium won't be distracted by what I call "monkey mind thoughts." These are the mind's attempt to make rational judgments. For example, let's say I'm a medium, and you come to me. I'm likely to immediately begin thinking about your age or appearance, or facial expressions. "Humm, she's about 50 so her mother is probably 75 so that means her mother probably liked Lawrence Welk . . . "

These thoughts are distractions and interfere with intuition.

The listing of mediums available at Windbridge.org on June 20, 2009—the day this page was type set—can be found on page 50.

Anecdotal Evidence of Communication with Discarnates

As mentioned above, mediums consistently report they feel a presence when doing a discarnate reading. They say they feel no such presence when doing a psychic reading for a living person. This has been described by one medium as the difference between "watching a play and reading a book."

Windbridge Certified Mediums
As of June 20, 2009

Samara Anjelae
Location: Kentucky
WCRM Level: 3
www.samarasays.com

Dave Campbell
Location: Arizona
WCRM Level: 3
www.theastrologystore.com

Joanne Gerber
Location: Massachusetts
WCRM Level: 3
www.joannegerber.com

Debra Martin
Location: Arizona
WCRM Level: 4
www.goldenmiracles.com

Doreen Molloy
Location: New Jersey
WCRM Level: 5
www.doreenmolloy.com

Stephanie A. Stevens
Location: Arizona
WCRM Level: 3
www.ommaster.com

Anyone who has experienced such a presence will know what the mediums mean by "presence." I wrote about one in my book *THE TRUTH*. Some years ago I experienced the presence of a deceased friend named Philippe, a man who had been engaged to one of my first wife's good friends named Joel. It happened at Joel's house in Marseilles, France.

Notre Dame Looks Down

The Ghost of Philippe Sirot

The house where Joel lived with her mother was situated on a steep, curved lane where walls hid quiet gardens, on the southern side of the hill below the Cathedral of Notre Dame, which is topped by a statue of the holy madonna. This icon of the mother of Jesus looks down from the highest point in that city. She has a magnificent view of the burning bright, azure harbor and the island fortress of Count of Monte Cristo fame. The house was a hundred feet or so directly below Mary's statue,

**Cathedral and Statue
from the Harbor**

behind an iron gate, recessed into the side of the hill. The stucco covered stone house had three levels, the bottom of which was an English basement at grade with a terrace. This had been turned into a separate apartment and rented out.

The first tenant turned out to be a dashing young man who worked with Jacques Cousteau (1910–1997). This young Frenchman, Philippe Sirot, gallivanted around the world on a converted minesweeper called the Calypso along with Cousteau and his motley ban of adventurers and marine biologists. The apartment in the quiet Marseilles neighborhood was where he lived when he wasn't gallivanting. As luck and love would have it, he and Joel fell for each other and got engaged. My first wife and I had chummed around with them before my wife and I were married, and when we two tied the knot, Philippe had been the French equivalent of my best man. She had been the maid of honor.

That had been in happier times. The mood was somber when we arrived at the house in Marseilles that year. Only a few months prior, the dashing young man had died a tragic death.

Philippe had been possessed of a fascination with death. He sincerely believed that it did not represent the end. Rather, he hypothesized that we enter another dimension, that we "cross over" into what I now realize is the mental world of spirit that in many respects mirrors the physical side of existence. Looking back with the perspective that time and increased knowledge give, I believe his preoccupation, his burning curiosity, may have led him to harbor an unconscious death wish. I recall vividly how he would barrel down a narrow Marseilles city street on a 750 cc Triumph motorcycle at 120 miles an hour. He did this once with me hanging on in back. You cannot imagine the sheer terror

I felt at the time. He also flew small planes, once taking a Piper Cub to Corsica across open water at night with no instruments.

Skydiving was another hobby, and deep sea diving was part of his job. You can still catch sight of Philippe on television, in reruns of *The Undersea World of Jacques Cousteau,* playing ring around the rosy with a bunch of hungry sharks.

Philippe Falls into Despair

In the year or two leading up to our visit to Marseilles that year, Philippe had fallen into despair, and his death was thought to have been the result of suicide.

Several things had gone wrong for him. First, by that time—the mid 1970s—Cousteau and the Calypso were no longer taking voyages to exotic locations. Replacing a job as a seafaring adventurer isn't easy. But he needed one, and he'd taken a position as captain of a boat that tended offshore oil rigs. The result was that he was bored to death, perhaps almost literally.

Second, his romance with Joel was on the rocks. From what I could determine, they'd broken up after a couple of silly arguments. She was still mad about him, but was playing a game some people play—hard to get. She refused to see him, no matter how he tried.

Who knows what else had gone wrong. Other factors may have come into play that I cannot recall or of which I was unaware. But the bottom line was, he was found dead one day in his cabin at sea.

Philippe Promises to Communicate with His Friends

On several occasions Philippe had told friends that he would communicate with them after he died if it were possible. This occurred to me as I paid the cab driver and collected our luggage.

Joel was all aflutter when we arrived. She was bursting to unload a lot of pent up stuff on my wife. For starters, her wristwatch had stopped when his funeral had begun, and had not resumed until the moment the funeral ended. I didn't see that this actually proved anything, but it did make me wonder. Anyway, I didn't have much opportunity to think because Joel was jabbering on and on about black cats and bumps in the night.

We all had a late dinner that evening, and I decided to turn in. My head was starting to ache from trying to keep up with the conversation, which was in French. It looked as though Joel and my wife were well on the way to staying up all night talking, so I suggested that I put our daughter Sophie to bed and then turn in myself.

Sophie was in another room, playing with her dolls. We said good night to her mom and Joel, descended a dark, circular staircase, and walked hand in hand through a dimly lit storage room. As in past years, we'd be sleeping in Philippe's old apartment. My hand closed around the knob and I pushed the door open.

Nothing had changed. Every piece of furniture, every wall hanging was exactly as he'd left it.

I Experience Philippe's Presence

The most bizarre sensation overwhelmed me. I felt that Philippe was there in the room, present among his belongings: the American Indian throw on the bed, the primitive masks and spears on the walls, the little statues and knickknacks from all over the world, including local deities and fertility gods. His presence was palpable, and it grew more so each second, seeming to close in on me, as if he had moved close to examine my face. I could almost feel his breath.

I did not want to upset my daughter, so I helped her into her pajamas, and went through the usual bedtime routine of a story. At last, I put her down in a child's bed, which had been positioned at the foot of Philippe's, and turned out the lights—except for one by the bed I'd use to read by. Then I crawled under the covers.

All was silent. I opened a book but could not concentrate. Philippe's presence was strong, particularly when I looked at the primitive wall hanging of a sunburst. The hand-woven image reminded me of the rising sun of Japan. My eyes were drawn to the center until the circle filled my vision.

What seemed a disembodied voice said, "Don't think about ghosts. It doesn't do any good to think about ghosts."

It was my daughter, Sophie. I'd thought she was asleep, but along with every hair on my body, she was sitting up.

I had no idea she even knew what a ghost was, or rather what a ghost was supposed to be. We'd never talked about them. At that point in my life, I wasn't sure they existed. I was still a materialist, not having come to the conclusion the world view I'd bought into was off base.

In retrospect I should have asked, "Why do you say that, dear?" But I wasn't thinking clearly. Instead, I said, "That's correct, dear. It doesn't do any good to think about ghosts." She laid down, and I didn't hear from her again that night.

What do you suppose caused her to sit up and make that rather interesting observation?

I have to wonder if Philippe wasn't fulfilling his promise and communicating with me through my three year old daughter's half asleep mind. Anyhow, the sense of his presence was undeniable and prevents me from dismissing the reports of psychics of feeling a presence during a chat with a discarnate.

The need for the actual presence of a discarnate may also be the reason psychics aren't able to conjure up discussions with dead historical figures such as Abraham Lincoln, George Washington or Napoleon Bonaparte. What would be in it for them to show up? Why should they? To make the cover of the *National Enquirer?*

On the other hand, my dead father might have been perfectly willing to come to a seance that would have given him the opportunity to assure me it wasn't my scribbling on the kitchen wall with magic marker, and his resulting fit of anger, that led to his coronary thrombosis.

Or, maybe he'd say it was.

Time for a New Paradigm

As previously discussed, besides continuation of consciousness after death, there are two other possible explanations for psychics' ability to give accurate information about the dead: the possible tapping into of a psychic reservoir, and what paranormal researchers call superpsi— the combination of clairvoyance, telepathy, remote viewing and so forth. Dr. Beischel joked that the only way to disprove the superpsi hypothesis when studying mediums is if they are able to retrieve information that never has and never will exist in the physical universe.

No matter which of the three possible explanations is correct, as in the case of NDEs and remote viewing, none fit the paradigm currently accepted by the majority of mainstream scientists today—the paradigm some have labeled "materialistic-reductionist science." This paradigm holds that the only reliable knowledge about the nature of the physical universe is that gained by the five ordinary senses. It rejects the notion that anything can survive the death of the body and has led to the erroneous and devastatingly harmful view held by practitioners of modern psychology that the brain is the seat of consciousness. The idea of a nonmaterial mind or soul that can survive death is held to be impossible.

How science stumbled off onto the wrong track will be discussed, but first let me explain how Dr. Beischel intends to determine if continuation of consciousness or one of the other two possibilities accounts for how mediums can report accurate information about discarnates.

Research on Discarnate Versus Living Person Readings

As mentioned, Dr. Beischel has gathered a good deal of qualitative as well as quantitative information concerning how mediums feel when they are conducting a reading with a discarnate—a presence; viewing a play—as opposed to how they feel while doing a reading for a living person, i.e., reading a book. She has published a peer reviewed paper about this.

Next, she plans to develop a research methodology wherein the psychic will be asked to give two readings, one to gather information from a discarnate, and the other about a living person. The psychic will not know which is which. All he or she will be given is a first name. Data concerning the psychic's feelings about the reading and the person they are gathering information about will be collected to see if there is statistically significant support for what the mediums have been reporting.

Dr. Beischel Communicates with Her Mom

You may be wondering, as I did during that first interview, if Dr. Beischel was able to contact her mother through a medium. She said she was—that she did so once. She said the session convinced her the medium was not employing telepathy to read her [Julie's] mind. The medium was talking about a brown station wagon her mother used to drive. Immediately, Julie recalled as a child having left a green crayon in that station wagon that melted into the carpet because of the Arizona heat.

Her mind screamed, *Green crayon! Green crayon!*

But the medium never said anything about a green crayon.

Perhaps the most convincing and certainly most dramatic contact with her deceased mother, however, was in the form of a dream. She had dreamed about her mother before, about seeing her with bags packed and leaving. That had been an ordinary dream. The convincing dream was one in which her mother spoke to her. It was vivid, lifelike and seemed absolutely real. I've had lucid dreams on occasion and I imagine that's what it was like. I did not ask the content of Dr. Beischel's dream, but apparently Julie got whatever answers she was looking for.

Communications with the Dead in the Dream State

Edgar Cayce (1877-1945)

The famous psychic Edgar Cayce, who gave more than 14,000 psychic readings, suggested a number of times that our loved ones who have passed away often try to communicate with us in the dream state. Dream researcher, Jody Long, who has been a guest on my radio show, believes being in the dream state may make it easier for loved ones who have passed to communicate with us. Our subconscious mind has its guard up in the waking state so that only a tiny amount of what is going on around us enters our consciousness. If this were not the case, we would simply be unable to process all the stimuli available to us. In the dream or drowsy state, however, our guard is down, lowering the threshold. This may make it easier to receive communications from the other side.

My apologies to regular listeners of my radio show who have heard me tell the story that follows, but I feel compelled to do so as it relates directly to receiving messages from the other side while in the dream or drowsy state. It has to do with an acquaintance of mine, a French count named Henri Dmitry. He told me this story about twenty-five years ago when my first wife and I were spending several days with him and his wife their chateau in Lorraine.

Henri had inherited his castle and the land and village around it along with his title—long after the castle had fallen into disrepair. It had not been lived in since before World War Two.

The Source of Night Noises Is Tracked Down

Having done well in business, Henri decided to restore the old place. He and his wife spend quite a bit of time there as it was undergoing renovation and were often disturbed in the middle of the night by what seemed to be someone down in the basement screaming. Inevitably, it would wake them up. At other times, they would hear the noise in that drowsy state as they were falling asleep or waking up. This happened almost every night. Finally, they became so annoyed, Henri had the workmen tear out a wall he judged to be the place from which the nocturnal uproar was emanating.

A skeleton was behind it.

Henri and his wife had no idea who the skeleton belonged to, but they gave it a Christian burial. Afterward, they were never again bothered by the night noises.

Here's what Henri thought about this. A man had been bricked up behind the wall while he was still alive—someone didn't like the guy. Maybe he'd been knocked on the head. Maybe he came to after the bricks were put in place. Then he died, but he did not realize it.

We will go into a full discussion of this phenomenon in an upcoming chapter. Suffice it to say the spirit of this dead person could easily have passed through the bricks, but the dead man didn't know this because he didn't know he was dead. He'd been calling for help ever since. Of course, these were psychic screams, since the ghost had no vocal cords. The middle of the night was the only time the screams for help penetrated the minds of Henri and his wife because that was when all else was quiet, and they were sleeping, or near sleep, and their minds were sensitive to such things.

The dead man didn't know how long he'd been trapped behind the bricks. People who have studied this sort of thing say time is not experienced in the spirit dimension. In an upcoming chapter we will learn why this is so.

There are more things in heaven and earth, Horatio,
than are dreamt of in your philosophy.

Shakespeare's Hamlet
(1564–1616)

Chapter Four
Evidence from the Past
Consciousness Continues

In August, 2008, I interviewed Stephen Braude, Ph.D., Editor-in-Chief of the *Journal of Scientific Exploration* and a professor of philosophy at the University of Maryland, Baltimore County. We talked about his book *IMMORTAL REMAINS: The Evidence for Life After Death*.

Stephen Braude, Ph.D.

Dr. Braude has been researching the paranormal for more than 30 years. I was curious to know how he got interested.

He said he was in graduate school and a hard nosed materialist at the time. He'd never really thought about things psychic. A couple of friends came over one day, looking for something to do, and suggested the three of them play a game called "Table Up."

It turned out this meant, "Let's have a seance."

For the next three hours, Dr. Braude watched his table rise in the air and spell out the answers to questions posed by him and his friends. Dr. Braude said that typically in these sorts of sessions, yes or no questions are asked. The table is asked to tilt once for yes and twice for no. But he and his friends didn't know this and asked open ended questions, telling the table to tilt once for the letter A, twice for B, three times for C and so forth. As you can imagine, this got rather tedious.

This happened in broad daylight. It happened in Dr. Braude's house. And his table did the tilting.

He added that none of the three of them were stoned.

He and both his friends would sometimes stand next to the table to verify no one's knees were doing the lifting. The table would still rise under their fingers.

Dr. Braude's curiosity was aroused by this session, and he has been studying the paranormal ever since. This has led to many run ins with pseudo skeptics, which may be the reason he knows just about every possible argument to shoot down the idea that mediums can communicate with the dead.

Unlike Julie Beischel, Stephen Braude does not to my knowledge conduct original research. He delves into eyewitness accounts from reliable witnesses that come from the heyday of spiritualism—the late nineteen and early twentieth centuries. At that time, many mediums were "trance mediums," which means a discarnate would take over their bodies and speak through them, using a medium's voice box and vocal cords to speak. Mediums no longer do this. You will understand why, later, when we delve into the topic of spirit possession.

Factors Professor Braude Uses to Judge Veracity of Claims

Professor Braude says he considers a number of factors to judge the veracity of reports of discarnates speaking through mediums. Some he calls the usual suspects: Mis-reporting, mal-observation, hidden memories, i.e., things people forgot about, or fraud. Then there are the unusual suspects: photographic memory, prodigies, idiot savants, and the remarkable things people can sometimes do when hypnotized.

But he doesn't stop there. Even if he finds a case that can't be explained by the usual or unusual suspects, that old bugaboo, psychic functioning among the living, otherwise known as superpsi, still looms. Obviously, people want to think their loved one survived and, when their time comes, they will survive death as well. Plus, the medium wants to satisfy a client. So what appears valid may simply be a good show put on by the medium, combined with a willing and credulous audience.

For this reason, he says the most convincing cases are those in which a discarnate drops into a seance and no one present knows the discarnate who has dropped in. This is especially true when the discarnate—communicating through the medium's voice box—does not give information that in any way supports or fulfills the needs or desires of anyone present. The most compelling are cases are when what the discarnate says makes sense only in terms of the discarnate's interests or agenda. For example, the discarnate may have unfinished business to take care of. Otherwise, why would he or she show up? Such cases do exist.

The Case of the Icelandic Drunkard

One related to me by Dr. Braude took place at a seance in Iceland. On several occasions, a trance medium's body was taken over by a "drop-in" discarnate with a drinking problem. The medium didn't drink, but that didn't stop the discarnate from repeatedly demanding alcohol while speaking through the medium's body to those present.

The discarnate gave information about himself that was later confirmed by a variety of sources. But most remarkable, he claimed to be looking for his leg.

First, he said his leg was in the sea. Then he said it was in the wall of a house belonging to one of those at the seance.

Later, research undertaken by the seance attendees found this man had been in a drunken stupor by the ocean, had fallen asleep, and was washed out to sea by the tide. His body eventually returned to shore, where it was torn to pieces by dogs and ravens.

Most of the man's bones were recovered and buried, but not all of them. The discarnate said a thighbone had not been buried and was in the wall of a house where one seance participant lived.

This participate later talked to the man who'd built his house and indeed found the builder had put a thighbone, a femur, in one wall. DNA testing did not exist back then so it wasn't possible to prove the femur actually belonged to the man. But the discarnate had been tall, and the femur in the wall had belonged to a tall man.

A Convincing Case of Reincarnation

When it comes to reincarnation, Dr. Braude has a keen eye for motives that might indicate fraud, and factors that seem to indicate superpsi or the psychic reservoir are not the sources of information. Among children who recall past lives, for example, this would include highly emotional reunions with relatives from the past life such as wives, husbands or children. He also looks for attitudes or knowledge that a child normally would not be expected to have.

He spoke of one convincing case—that of a young boy in India who claimed to be the reincarnation of a man who had lived quite some distance away. The man he claimed to have been had lived a life of debauchery and had carried on extensively with a prostitute. After his rebirth, and having achieved the ripe old age of three, he advised his father to get himself a mistress.

His father asked why.

The child replied that he would have much pleasure from her, and went into some detail about what he meant by pleasure—not the sort of thing one would expect to hear from a three year old.

Body Parts Contain Urges and Desires

Dr. Braude also talked about transplant cases. These are situations where a heart or kidneys or some other organ is transplanted and the recipient starts having feelings and cravings that seem to have belonged to the organ donor. This indicates the brain is not the only physical link to our desires and preferences. Dr. Braude told the story of a young man who received a heart-lung transplant from a lesbian painter. After his recovery from the surgery, his girlfriend reported that his personality had changed dramatically. He now enjoyed hanging out in art galleries, he seemed to have developed an understanding of and deep appreciation for landscape paintings, and perhaps most interesting, his lovemaking was completely different. He showed a definite appreciation and understanding of female anatomy that he had not possessed before.

The Little Lady Who Craved Chicken Nuggets & Beer

I learned of another case from a different source. After a heart transplant, a lady began having constant cravings for chicken nuggets and beer. This was odd because she'd never had chicken nuggets before, and she didn't drink beer or any other kind of alcoholic beverage—at least not before her surgery. After a having a recurring dream in which a young man came to her saying he loved her and had given her his heart, she decided to find out who her new heart had come from. Following a good deal of detective work, she learned it had belonged to a young man, the victim of a motorcycle crash, who'd been found with a box of MacDonald's chicken nuggets and a six pack of beer stuffed inside his motorcycle jacket.

The Lumberjack Who Liked Housework & Knitting

Here's another case. Back on January 17, 2006—I know the date because I jotted it down—I took a lunch break from writing *A Witch in the Family,* a book about my ancestor, Susannah North Martin, who was hanged as a witch in Salem, Massachusetts, in 1692. While eating, I watched a series of online video clips at a news web site. One of these reported on a Croatian lumberjack who had received a lifesaving kidney transplant and now was suing the hospital that gave it to him. The man's favorite pastime had once been spending time in the local pub, carousing with his buddies. Now, he had developed a passion for housework and knitting. This had made him the laughing stock of his village. He believed the kidney was to blame, and he was probably right. The donor was a 51 year-old-woman.

I asked Dr. Braude what was the most convincing case he'd come across. He said it was that of Leonora Piper, who for many years consistently gave accurate readings to loved ones and to proxies of loved ones about discarnates.

The Case of Leonora Simonds Piper

Leonora Simonds Piper was born in Nashua, New Hampshire in June 1859. Her first inkling toward her future career occurred when she was only eight years-old, playing in the garden. She felt a sharp pain in her right ear and a whispered voice said, "Aunt Sara, not dead, but with you still."

Leonora Simonds Piper (1859-1950)

Terrified, Leonora ran into the house and told her mother. They found out later her Aunt Sara had died at about the moment this had occurred.

Leonora's mediumship began in earnest in 1884 after her father-in-law took her for a medical consultation with J.R. Cook, a blind clairvoyant who had a reputation for diagnosing illnesses and suggesting cures. Leonora lost consciousness at Cook's touch and entered a trance. Later, she attended a home circle sitting, otherwise known as a seance, and entered a trance in which she produced a message for someone present. The person considered the message to be the most accurate he had received during his 30 year interest in Spiritualism.

It wasn't long before Leonora began giving private seances in her home. This is how she became acquainted with Professor William James of Harvard, a founder of the Pragmatic School of Thought, which held that only those principles that can be demonstrated—not only theoretically but practically—deserve intelligent consideration. Even though he was an unbending pragmatist, he was converted by Leonora to a belief in psychic phenomena to such a degree that he became one of the founding members of the American Society for Psychical Research (ASPR).

Leonora came to Professor James' attention through his mother-in-law, a Mrs. Gibbens, who heard about her through friends and decided to schedule an appointment. After her meeting with Piper, she returned to the James' home and told the professor that in a trance, Piper had told her facts about relatives, living and dead, she could not have possibly have known in any normal way. James laughed and called Mrs. Gibbens a "victim" of a medium's trickery. He gave her an explanation as to how mediums accomplished their fraud, but Mrs. Gibbens refused to consider this and returned for another seance the following week. This time, she convinced James' sister-in-law to accompany her. After this visit, the two women insisted James visit the medium himself, and he agreed.

When James arrived at the Piper home, he was surprised to find the complete absence of Spiritualist props—no cabinet, no red lights, circles of chairs, trumpets or bells. The sitters, of which there were two or three others present, merely sat wherever they liked in the Piper's living room. In addition, Leonora herself was not what James had expected. She was quiet and shy—there was nothing flamboyant about her. She politely warned her guests that there would be nothing sensational about the seance—they should not expect any dishes or plates to fly about. She would simply go into a trance and one of her spirit controls would then take over. There might or might not be messages given—she had no control over that.

James was impressed with what he saw. Leonora was able to summon up the names of his wife's father and even that of a child that he and his wife had lost the previous year. He gave Piper no information to work with and in fact, was purposely quiet throughout the seance.

He later wrote, "My impression after this first visit was that Mrs. Piper was either possessed of supernormal powers or knew the members of my wife's family by sight and had by some lucky coincidence become acquainted with such a multitude of their domestic circumstances as to produce the startling impression which she did. My later knowledge of her sittings and personal acquaintance with her has led me to absolutely reject the latter explanation, and to believe that she has supernormal powers."

James was stumped and made appointments for 25 of his friends to visit her, thus starting research that would continue for the remainder of Leonora's career. Piper's talent was considered to be so extraordinary that she was taken to England for 83 sittings with men considered to be the premiere psychical researchers of the day, including Henry Sidgwick, Sir Oliver Lodge, Sir William Barrett, F.W.H. Meyers and Dr. Walter Leaf. Although she was in a place she'd never been before, was closely watched, and even consented to having her mail opened, Piper did extremely well and continued to amaze even the most hardened investigators.

Nevertheless, it seems to me that even though fraud might have been impossible, she could have been accessing the psychic reservoir or employing superpsi. Some of what we will take a look at in the next chapter, however, cannot possibly be explained by such psychic powers. Continuation of consciousness after death is the only logical explanation.

Chapter Five
Almost Fifty Years of Irrefutable Research

Suppose you were changing your son's diaper—let's say he was just beginning to talk and was quite verbally adept at the age of 18 months—and he looked you in the eye and said, "When I was your age, I used to change your diaper."

What would you think?

If your father happened to be deceased, would you possibly think your son might be your father reincarnated? That would make him his own grandfather.

Can something like that happen?

Jim B. Tucker, M.D.

I spoke with someone on my radio show in March 2009 who seems to think so. His name is Jim B. Tucker and he his not a wild-eyed Looney Tune. He's a Phi Beta Kappa graduate of the University of North Carolina, a medical doctor, and a board certified child psychiatrist who serves as medical director of the Child & Family Psychiatry Clinic at the University of Virginia School of Medicine. Dr. Tucker has been studying this possibility in a serious and scientific way.

The University of Virginia Medical School—in what is now known as its Division of Perceptual Studies—has been researching the subject of children's memories of past lives since 1961. Much of this work was done by, or under direction of, the late Ian Stevenson, M.D. (1918-2007), who wrote a shelf full of books on the subject, having compiled more than 2500 such cases. About 1600 of these have been

**The Rotunda at
The University of Virginia**

entered into a computer data base along with the information collected on each. This has been sorted into about 200 different variables, allowing researchers to comb through and cross tabulate the data to spot trends as well as to categorize and compare the similarities and differences based on various factors and characteristics.

**Ian Stevenson, M.D.
(1918-2007)**

Dr. Stevenson was a methodical and meticulous researcher who graduated first in his medical school class at Canada's McGill University. He never actually claimed reincarnation as fact, but rather, said his cases were "suggestive" of reincarnation. His often-cited first book on the subject was published in 1966 and entitled, *Twenty Cases Suggestive of Reincarnation.*

The cases he studied come from all over the world. When Dr. Stevenson began this research, they were easiest to find in places where people have a belief in reincarnation such as

India and Thailand. This may be because parents were not as likely to think a child was imagining a past life, and because they are not likely to be embarrassed to talk about it. Nowadays, however, people in the United States are not as reticent as they once were. Dr. Tucker says that since the University of Virginia set up a web site on this subject ten years ago, he and his colleagues hear from parents "all the time" about their children's memories of past lives.

Nevertheless, in the United States reincarnation is thought by many to go against Christian doctrine, even though recent surveys show that more than twenty percent of Christians believe in reincarnation. The percentage is higher, by the way, among younger adults.

Reincarnation and Christianity

I'd like devout Christians who may be reading this to know about a man I interviewed on my radio show in the spring of 2008. His name is James A. Reid Sr., and he's a Southern Baptist minister, now retired. He holds a Doctor of Ministry degree from San Francisco Theological Seminary. For 15 years he was Chaplain to the Los Vegas strip, where he heard a lot of talk about Edgar Cayce and past lives, which he always dismissed as fantasy thinking. Finally, he got so fed up he decided to write a book denouncing reincarnation as a Biblically untenable doctrine. But Dr. Reid is an honest and mature individual. Once he dug into Church history and the Scriptures, he was forced to change his view. He ended up writing a book that maintains the Bible supports the doctrine of reincarnation. It is called, *BORN AGAIN AND AGAIN AND AGAIN: A Bible-Based View of Reincarnation.*

Reincarnation Was Accepted for 500 Years

Dr. Reid maintains that for the first five hundred year history of the Church, reincarnation was accepted as fact by many. It wasn't until 553 A.D. that it was condemned by the Council of Constantinople, and then only by a narrow margin. He gives several examples indicating Jesus and others of his time believed in reincarnation. For example, John the Baptist was supposed by many to be the prophet Elijah reincarnated. Jesus himself said this was so. (See Matthew 11:14.) Once, Jesus asked his followers who people thought he (Jesus) was. They replied that many believed him (Jesus) to be one of the prophets—presumably reincarnated, since the last prophet died about 400 years earlier. Also, consider the story of Jesus healing the blind man as recounted in John 9:1-12, which begins as follows:

> *As he went along, he saw a man blind from birth.*
> *His disciples asked him, 'Rabbi, who sinned, this man*
> *or his parents, that he was born blind?'*
> *'Neither this man nor his parents sinned,' said*
> *Jesus, 'but this happened so that the work of God*
> *might be displayed in his life.'*

Since the man was blind from birth, the only way his sins could have caused his blindness was for him to have sinned in a former life. Jesus did not tell his followers this wasn't possible. To the contrary, he seems to have assumed it was possible, although he gives another reason for the man's blindness, saying, "Neither this man nor his parents sinned, but this happened so that the work of God might be displayed in his life."

Edgar Cayce, whose psychic readings probably did more than anything to promote the concept of reincarnation in the West, was a devout Presbyterian and Sunday school teacher who read the Bible once through for every year of his life. At first, when reincarnation started showing up in his readings, he was baffled and confused. But he reread the Bible and satisfied himself it wasn't anti-Christian.

There are many references to reincarnation in the Bible but believers overlook or misinterpret them because they have been conditioned to think reincarnation is taboo. Kevin Todeschi, Executive Director of the Association for Research and Enlightenment, said on my radio show in November, 2007, that he has counted eleven such references in Matthew's gospel alone.

Reincarnation Does Not Conflict with Jesus's Teachings

As a regular churchgoer myself, and a follower of Jesus, it's my personal opinion nothing about reincarnation is incompatible with Jesus' message and what he set out to accomplish. Read the Gospels. What he was trying to tell us isn't at all complicated. He put it succinctly in John 15:17: "This is my command: Love each other."

Jesus' main objective is also pretty clear. It's to bring heaven to earth. He talks about this constantly and uses parables to explain what heaven is. For instance, this verse (Matthew 13:44) indicates how wonderful it would be: "The kingdom of heaven is like a treasure hidden in a field. When a man found it, he hid it again, and then in his joy went and sold all he had and bought that field."

Bringing heaven to earth is one of the main points of the prayer Jesus taught that practically everyone in Christendom knows by heart:

". . . *Thy kingdom come,* Thy will be done, *on earth as it is in heaven . . .* "

And how does one bring the kingdom of heaven to earth? By loving God first—rather than stuff like money—and by loving his neighbor as himself. By treating others as he would like and hope to be treated, as in the parable of the good Samaritan. Imagine if everyone did that. . . .

Wouldn't it bring heaven to earth?

The Child Who Is His Grandfather

In the case mentioned at the beginning of this chapter—the 18 month old child who said he had changed his father's diaper when he was his father's age—the child's mother was the daughter of a Southern Baptist preacher. As you might imagine, she found what her son said to be highly unusual. I asked Dr. Tucker to describe the case when he came on my show, and he obliged.

The child's grandfather had died eighteen months before the child's birth. His first mention of having been his own grandfather was during that change of diapers, but as time went by he made more comments about how he used to be big, and what he did when he was. His mother in particular became interested and began to ask the boy, whose name was Sam, questions. Sam came up with some very specific statements. For instance, she asked him if he had had any bothers or sisters. He said he had had a sister who was killed. In fact the grandfather's sister had been murdered sixty years before.

The parents felt certain the child could not have known this since they had only recently learned about it themselves.

The child also talked about how, at the end of his previous life, his wife would make milkshakes for him every day, and that she made them in a food processor rather than in a blender. This turned out to be true.

When Sam was four years old, his grandmother—his wife in his previous life—died. Sam's dad traveled to where she lived and took care of the estate. When he returned, he brought some family photos with him.

One night Sam's mother had the pictures spread out on the coffee table. Sam walked over and pointed to pictures of his grandfather and said, "Hey, that's me."

To test him she pulled out a class photo from the time the grandfather was in elementary school. Sam ran his finger across the photo, which had sixteen boys in it, and stopped on the one who had indeed been his grandfather.

"That's me," he said.

The Reason Sam May Have Come Back

The grandfather may have come back as the son of his own son because of the relationship—or lack thereof—the two had had in his previous life. The grandfather had not had an open relation with Sam's dad. He had been a very private person. Sam's dad felt that if his father had really returned as his son, his father may have decided to come back to try to develop a closer bond than had existed in their previous relationship. Dr. Tucker said this may be true. When he visited the family he could see that Sam and his dad were very close.

A Dad Determined to Be Reborn

A similar case was told to me by a successful lawyer friend who wishes to remain anonymous. I'll call him Frank. If his story is true—and I have no reason to doubt it—it demonstrates the tenacity a soul can have if it wishes to incarnate and be close to a specific person.

Frank was divorced. He had two children from the marriage and no intention of having any more—even if he should remarry. One night he had a dream, a very vivid dream such as the one Julie Beischel had when her mother came to her. In his case, Frank's dream was about his father—with whom he had been very close. But his father didn't actually visit him face to face. He called Frank on the phone.

The dream seemed very real and was crystal clear. It took place at Frank's office. As he was talking to his dad, Frank recalled his secretary telling someone who wanted to see him not to interrupt.

"Frank's talking with his father."

"Isn't his father dead?"

"Yes," the secretary said. "But you know Frank. He probably really is talking to his father. You can't go in there."

Frank and his father had quite a conversation—one that went on for some time. They had a lot to catch up about because Frank's father had been dead for a number of years.

At one point in the conversation, as it was coming to an end, Frank said, "I'm glad you called, Dad. I miss you."

The father replied, "I miss you, too, son. But you know, it may not be as long as you might think before we're together again."

"Uh-oh," Frank said. "Is something going to happen to me?"

"Oh, no, don't worry, son," the father said. "Nothing is going to happen to you."

As you recall, Frank was divorced. But he did have a girlfriend, and you need to know something else in order to fully appreciate this story. Frank had had a disease of the testes that had left him almost sterile—though not completely. He had an extremely low sperm count—about ten percent of normal. He'd been told by his doctor it was highly unlikely he'd ever have more children.

Nevertheless, his girlfriend always took precautions, including the use of a diaphragm and spermicide. But, as you may have guessed, she became pregnant. And you know what? She had a premonition the baby she was carrying was Frank's father—Frank's father's soul—about to reincarnate.

After a good deal of agonizing and debate, she decided to have the pregnancy terminated. Not long afterwards, perhaps because of the disharmony her decision caused, Frank moved on and found another girlfriend.

You guessed it, the next girlfriend also became pregnant—despite what would normally have been ample precautions.

The second girlfriend had her pregnancy terminated.

Keep in mind that Frank was virtually sterile, and they always used birth control because—miraculously, it seemed—the same woman became pregnant a second time. When this happened Frank concluded nothing was going to stop the soul on the other side—the soul who wanted to come through and have him as father. He begged the young woman to go through with the pregnancy.

But she refused and the fetus was aborted, thus ending their relationship.

Shortly afterwards, Frank had another dream—a very vivid dream. He dreamt that he went up to the attic of his house and discovered three little girls there.

Parenthetically, let me say the majority of those who have studied reincarnation, those I've spoken with, believe souls are androgynous—they have no sex—and can incarnate either as males or females.

In his dream about the attic, Frank encountered not boys, but three little girls. One was several years old—the age the baby born of the first pregnancy would have been had she come to term. The second was the age the child of the next pregnancy, and the third was a tiny infant—the age of the third.

In Frank's dream he became enraged and upset upon finding these children in his attic. He lost his temper, found a baseball bat and beat them with it.

Afterwards, still dreaming, Frank's anger dissipated and a sense of terrible remorse came over him. As he sobbed uncontrollably, one of the little girls attempted to console him. Touching his arm, she said, "Don't worry, you didn't hurt us. You can't hurt us. We're already dead."

A Little Girl Recognizes Frank

A few years later, Frank met a woman through his work who had a daughter about one year of age. The little girl's father had died suddenly and unexpectedly before she was born.

Frank thought the woman was attractive and accepted her invitation to come to dinner at her house.

When Frank arrived, the woman was all smiles.

"You look happy," he said as she stepped aside to let him into her house.

"I am," she said. "My daughter just said her first word."

"What was it?" Frank said.

"She said, 'Mamma.'"

Frank entered the house and saw the little girl.

He crouched down to talk to her.

The little girl looked up at him—into his eyes—and with feeling said, "Dadda!"

You guessed it. Frank and the woman were married.

Later, when the little girl was about two years old, she said to her mom one night when the mom was putting her to bed, "You know, Mom, I'm having trouble remembering."

"What are you having trouble remembering, dear?"

"I remember before, when I was big. And I remember Daddy then. But I don't remember you then—before, when I was big."

Later on, the little girl said a number of other, similar things Frank thinks indicate she was his father reincarnated. She also apparently displayed a number of his father's traits, including peculiar food preferences.

At this writing she is a senior in high school. She and Frank still have a close relationship, but she no longer recalls the time before—when she was big.

A Murder Victim Comes Back

Returning now to the files of the University of Virginia, another interesting case Dr. Tucker related on my show has to do with and Indian girl named Kum Kum, who said she had been murdered in her previous life—poisoned—by her daughter-in-law. Kum Kum said she was from a city of about 200,000 located about 25 miles away. One of the things that makes this a good case is that her aunt wrote down a number of statements—eighteen in all—she made before an effort was undertaken to see if they checked out.

All of them did.

The statements included the name of a son, the name of a grandson, the fact that the son had worked with a hammer. And a number of other specifics—for example, that she had a sword hanging near the cot where she slept, and a pet snake she fed milk to.

Research led to the woman Kum Kum claimed to have been, who had died five years before she was born. A big family flap had taken place over a will and who would inherit the worldly possessions of the deceased woman's son. Kum Kum had probably been right. Circumstantial evidence indicated the son's wife had poisoned her mother-in-law—the woman Kum Kum insisted she'd been.

What Many Cases Have in Common

These case histories are fascinating and convincing, and we could go on almost indefinitely considering them, individually. After all, there are more than 2500 in UVA's files that have checked out. Instead, let's step back and look at the overall findings of this exhaustive study.

Children who report past-life memories typically begin talking about a previous life when they are two to three years old. You may recall that Dr. Braude said emotional involvement with past-life family members would indicate reincarnation rather than superpsi or the psychic reservoir at work. Well, the children tend to show strong emotional involvement with such memories and often tearfully ask to be taken to the previous family. Once there, not only is a deceased individual usually identified whose life matched the details given, during the visits, children often recognize family members or friends from that individual's life. Tearful reunions are common.

Birthmarks and Birth Defects Provide Evidence

Many children studied also had birthmarks that matched wounds on the body of the deceased individual. To give one example, a boy in Thailand, who said he'd been a school teacher in this previous life, was shot and killed when riding his bicycle to school one day. He gave specific details including his name in that life and where he had lived. He continued to make this claim until his grandmother took him to the previous address. The child was able to identify the various members of his previous family by name.

Even more startling, however, he was born with two birth marks: a small round birthmark on the back of his head and a larger, more irregularly shaped one near the front. The woman he claimed was his wife in that life recalled investigators saying her husband had been shot from behind. The investigators said they knew this because he had a typical, small, round entrance wound in the back of his head and a larger, irregular exit wound in front.

In another case, a boy remembered a life in a village not far away in which he had lost the fingers of his right hand in a fodder chopping machine. The child was born with an intact left hand but the fingers of his right hand were missing.

The average length of time between the death and rebirth of the children in these birthmark cases is only fifteen to sixteen months. As we will see, this sort of thing may happen when the soul takes a short-cut between lives, skipping a process by which the life just lived would have been fully integrated into the soul.

Twenty-Two Percent of UVA Cases Have Birth Defects

According to Dr. Tucker's book, *Life Before Life* (St. Martin's Griffin, 2005), about 22 percent of the cases in the University's data base include birth defects due to wounds suffered in violent deaths in the previous life. Most of the cases come from the Hindu and Buddhist countries of South Asia, the Shiite peoples of Lebanon and Turkey, the tribes of West Africa, and the tribes of northwestern North America.

In 1997 Stevenson published details of 225 cases in a massive work

Reincarnation and Biology: A Contribution to the Etiology of Birthmarks and Birth Defects. The same year he presented a summary of 112 cases in a much shorter book, *Where Reincarnation and Biology Intersect.*

In many cases postmortem reports, hospital records, or other documents were located and consulted that confirmed the location of the wounds on the deceased person in question matched the birthmarks. These often correspond to bullet wounds or stab wounds, and as in the case described above. Sometimes two marks correspond to the points where a bullet entered and then exited the body.

Birthmarks also related to a variety of other wounds or marks, not necessarily connected with the previous personality's death, including surgical incisions and blood left on the body when it was cremated. A woman run over by a train that sliced her right leg in two was reborn with her right leg absent from just below the knee. A man born with a severely malformed ear had been resting in a field at twilight, mistaken for a rabbit, and shot in the ear.

Behavior Traits Also Provide Evidence

Further evidence for reincarnation comes from what might be called behavioral memories. For example, cases exist where children of lower caste Indian families believe they had been upper class Brahmins, and in their view still were. These children would refuse to eat their family's food, which they considered polluted. Conversely, a child remembering the life of a street-sweeper—a very low caste—showed an alarming lack of concern about cleanliness. Some children demonstrate skills they have not learned in their present life, but which the previous personality was known to have had. A number of Burmese children who recalled being Japanese soldiers killed there during World War Two preferred Japanese food such as raw or semi-raw fish over the spicy Burmese fair served by their families.

Many children express memories of the previous life in the games they play. A girl who remembered a previous life as a schoolteacher would assemble her playmates as pupils and instruct them with an imaginary blackboard. A child who remembered the life of a garage mechanic would spend hours under a family sofa "repairing" the car he pretended it to be. One child who remembered a life in which he had committed suicide by hanging himself had the habit of walking around with a piece of rope tied round his neck.

Phobias May Originate in a Former Life

Phobias occur in about a third of the cases and are nearly always related to the mode of death in the previous life. For example, death by drowning may lead to fear of being immersed in water; death from a snake bite may lead to a phobia of snakes; a child who remembers a life that ended when he was shot may display a phobia of guns and loud noises. A person who died in a traffic accident may have a phobia of cars, buses, or trucks.

Sexual orientation may also be affected by a previous life. In one of his books, Ian Stevenson wrote, "Such children almost invariably show traits of the sex of the claimed in the previous life. They cross-dress, play the games of the opposite sex, and may otherwise show attitudes characteristic of that sex. As with the phobias, the attachment to the sex and habits of the previous life usually becomes attenuated as the child grows older; but a few of these children remain intransigently fixed to the sex of the previous life, and one has become homosexual."

Certain preferences and cravings can also carry over. They frequently take the form of a desire or demand for particular foods not eaten in the child's present family, or for clothes different from those ordinarily worn by the family members. Other examples include cravings for addictive substances, such as tobacco, alcohol, and other drugs that the previous personality was known to have used.

UVA's Cases May Not Be Representative of the Whole

Dr. Tucker pointed out that the cases he and others have studied may not be typical because most children do not remember past lives. As mentioned, the average time between lives in these cases is only fifteen months or so—although there are outliers that range up to fifty years. In 70 percent of these cases, the previous personality died by unnatural means. Many died young. This may speed up the reincarnation process. The consciousness may come back quickly due to unfinished business, or because he or she feels shortchanged. The quick return may also be the reason past life memories are intact, as well as sexual preferences, cravings and so forth. My guess is that a much longer duration between lives is the norm.

Teachings of the Rosicrucians, a mystical order of which I have been a member, say the human personality span is normally about 140 years. If we live 70 years, for example, we can expect to spend 70 years in the realm between lives before we incarnate again. If we live 60 years, we can expect to spend 80 years between lives. The teachings stress, however, that this is a rule of thumb. Centuries could elapse between incarnations, or as with many in the UVA study, the return could come in a matter of months.

Children Aren't the Only Ones Who Have Past Life Memories

Memories of past lives also sometimes occur in adults, and such memories can be of lives that took place long ago. I once recalled a romantic interlude from a life as a Russian army officer during the Napoleonic Wars. It happened when I met the same woman in this life. A guest on my show recalled having a spontaneous recollection of a life as a woman that took place in twelfth or thirteenth century France. He was being burned at the stake. He said this was so vivid it seemed more than a memory. He actually felt he was there, subjectively experiencing the ordeal.

He'd been meditating when suddenly it seemed he was back in the skin he'd occupied then—the action taking place around him. Information about who he was and what was taking place was present in his mind as though he had literally been transported back in time and reentered that body. He said that, surprisingly, he did not feel much pain at being burned—his consciousness exited his body as soon as the flames engulfed it. He floated nearby observing his body burn—not feeling any pain at all. Nevertheless, it was a gut wrenching, emotional experience that left him so distraught he secluded himself after reliving the experience and was unable to communicate with others for two or three days.

He said his need to withdraw had not been because of the pain he'd endured. It was a result of the distress he felt over the pain and suffering humanity puts itself through—man's inhumanity to man. He'd been been burned at the stake in that life because he'd been a priestess of the Cathar religion, a gnostic Christian sect persecuted and eventually extinguished by the Roman Catholic Church. His death by fire was just one of many that took place during the twelfth through fourteenth centuries.

Why were these people killed? No doubt they were seen as a threat to those in power, which at that time included leaders of the Church. The Church taught and teaches that salvation comes through belief in Christ and his sacrifice on the cross. Gnostics followed Christ's teachings but believed salvation comes through direct knowledge of God—a direct and personal relationship. Today, this direct relationship is fostered by many if not all churches—a daily walk with God is considered a requisite by most. Catholicism in the time of the Cathars, however, taught that only the clergy could have this direct relationship.

A Memory Is Triggered of an Execution at Auschwitz

The same man recalled another past life triggered by a train trip he took in Poland. As the train moved out of the station in Warsaw, memories came cashing down upon him of a lifetime that had ended directly prior to this one. He'd been a Polish Jew—a boy in World War Two.

He was seven years old and an orphan when the Nazis invaded Poland and was swept up and placed in the Warsaw ghetto. He managed to survive as a street urchin for about four years. Then he was rounded up and driven along with other Jews into one of many boxcars of a train headed to Auschwitz.

He recalls vividly what happened next. When the prisoners exited the boxcars, the strong and healthy were herded off in one direction—to perform forced labor, he now assumes. The old and the young—into which category he fell—were taken immediately in a different direction to the "delousing center." There, they were told to remove their clothes and enter a room. About 200 to 250 crowded into a space and packed together like Tokyo commuters on a train. The room, of course, turned out to be a gas chamber, and it wasn't long before lethal gas emerged from the shower heads.

A Quick Exit of the Body and the Instinct to Help Others

Unlike many of those around him, when the poison began to take hold he left his body almost immediately and without much pain. He recalls vividly that many in the chamber were not willing or were unable to accept their deaths, continuing to believe they were there being deloused even after their bodies had died. In addition, there were hundreds, perhaps even thousands of disembodied spirits stuck there from prior mass executions. Instinctively, he seemed to understand their predicament and held back from entering the tunnel of light. Rather, he stayed behind and was able to help many move along.

Before he left, he was able to help several hundred move to the light. Once enough of the group had caught on to the fact they were dead and needed to move on, the word seemed to spread to others. He was able to both lead and push a sort of daisy chain of souls into and through the tunnel and on to the light.

Getting stuck after death seems to be fairly common, and it's something we all should be concerned about. In many cases, a soul does not realize its body is dead, or can't believe it, and remains in denial. We may be better off to see death coming.

This will be discussed in an upcoming chapter.

I sent my soul through the invisible, some letter of the afterlife to spell, and by and by my soul returned to me, and answered, I myself and heaven and hell.

Omar Khayyam
(1048-1122)

Chapter Six
Life Between Lives

As stated in the previous chapter, cases of reincarnation studied by the University of Virginia may not reflect what normally occurs when someone dies and reincarnates. This may be because most of the UVA cases have to do with souls that reincarnated after a violent death, or a death that came about unexpectedly. The experience of souls in these situations may be very different than that of others who lived a normal length of time, accomplished what they had intended in life, could see the end coming, and were able to prepare for death.

As has been discussed, many who have near death experiences, for example, report passing through what seems a corridor, or a tunnel and into the light where they are often greeted by archetypes or religious figures, and loved ones who have gone before. Some undergo a life review and counseling by entities they believe to be ascended masters and guides. This is not so in most of the cases studied by UVA. In one I read about many years ago, I believe it was in Dr. Stevenson's first book, the reincarnated entity had been attacked in his home by thieves, bound hand and foot with wire, and left to die. He floated out of his body and drifting around the neighborhood until he stumbled upon an opportunity to be reborn. He entered a fetus in his future mother's womb and never encountered a tunnel or saw a light. In his new life, he had birthmarks on his wrists and ankles where his hands and feet had been bound.

It seems possible that in many of the UVA cases some sort of normal progression between lives was skipped. Perhaps some souls who die a normal death and pass through the tunnel and into the light do not reincarnate at all. Maybe others do, but only after a number of steps have been taken, or stages have been passed through. This progression could be what causes memories to be absorbed or incorporated into a person's soul so that, once reborn, past life memories are no longer easily accessed. One may have to know one has died and fully process the former life in order to move past it and start fresh in a new one.

The Five Psychological Stages Preceding Death

In her book, *On Death & Dying* (Simon & Schuster/Collier Books, 1970), Elizabeth Kübler-Ross, M.D., wrote that terminally ill patients typically pass through five stages as they approach their demise: Denial, anger, bargaining, depression, and finally, acceptance. It should not be surprising, then, that many who die unexpectedly remain in the denial stage even after death. This is supported by findings of The Monroe Institute, the organization mentioned in an earlier chapter that was hired by the United States Government to train remote viewers.

TMI uses a protocol for inducing out-of-body experiences that visitors to weekend retreats and seminars offered by the Institute can try for themselves. Some are successful at achieving out-of-body travel and others are not. Some individuals become very adept at this.

How the Phenomenon of Stuck Souls Was Discovered

In a journey out of the body twenty or so years ago, one of these adepts came across the soul of an English sailor who, in the late 1840s, had died in a ship wreck at sea. The case is similar to the one recounted earlier of a man who had been bricked up behind a wall in the basement of a chateaux in Lorraine. Both men had died and didn't know it with the result they continued pursuing the activity they had been engaged in at the moment of death. In the case of the ghost of Henri's chateaux, this involved screaming for help from behind the brick wall that trapped him. In the case of the British sailor, it involved clinging to a piece of debris from the wreckage of his ship somewhere in the Irish sea—a ship that had gone down in a raging storm after putting out from Liverpool.

The adept from The Monroe Institute who came upon this soul was part of what was called the Explorer Program. In Explorer sessions, the adept places him or herself inside a specially designed sensory depravation chamber. The out-of-body experience (OBE) is initiated through the sound technology developed by Robert Monroe. The explorer wears ear phones, as was the case related earlier about Skip Atwater. A conversation takes place. Communication back and forth between the monitor and the OBE traveler is monitored and recorded.

In the case of the sailor in the Irish sea, the monitor could hear the conversation between the OBE explorer and the sailor—the adept's words to the sailor, and the sailor's responses relayed by the adept.

Time is not experienced in the sub atomic realm of spirit where this was taking place. We will cover why this is so when we review the theories of Thomas Troward in an upcoming chapter. The sailor did not know he'd been clinging to the ship's debris for more than 140 years. His mind created the situation he believed himself to be experiencing. For him, the ship wreck had happened a few hours earlier. The OBE explorer, of course, knew otherwise. She was fully aware more than 140 years must have passed, and his spirit must be stuck. With advice from the monitor listening in, the OBE researcher convinced the ship-wrecked sailor of his true situation and send him to the light.

TMI researchers now believe this the sort of thing is common and is the basis of many hauntings. Someone may die in a house, for example, and either not want to leave or not know he or she is dead.

The Lifeline Program Is Developed

After this episode, Robert Monroe did quite a bit of out-of-body exploring on his own to find out more about this phenomenon. He wrote about his explorations in his book, *The Ultimate Journey* (Main Street Books, 1996).

An unexpected or violent death is not the only reason souls get stuck. Some are caught up in materialistic ideas and pursuits and have no idea anything spiritual exists. This may happen to the pseudo skeptics who maintain doggedly, even in the face of scientific evidence to the contrary, that nothing exists that is not available to the five physical senses. They may never think to look for the tunnel and the light. Others, who see the tunnel and the light, may avoid going to it out of fear of what they may encounter—judgment for their transgressions.

A Psychiatrist Helps Stuck Souls See the Light

A while back I interviewed Shakuntala Modi, M.D., a psychiatrist who specializes in ridding people of earthbound spirits who attach themselves to the living and cause all manner of problems, both physical and mental. Her book is called *Remarkable Healings: A Psychiatrist Discovers Unsuspected Roots of Mental and Physical Illness* (Hampton Roads, 1998). Essentially, she speaks with these spirits through her hypnotized patients and attempts to convince them, usually with success, they should look up, see the light, and go to it. She tells them they will find comfort there and that no one other than themselves will judge them.

Spirit Possession Happens More Than You May Think

Some readers will find it difficult to believe spirit possession is real, even though references to it in literature go back thousands of years. Think about it. If some spirits remain on the earth plane after death, why should it be unusual for them to attach themselves to the living?

A soul entering a fetus may even be a form of possession. Of course, this must happen at conception. Otherwise, how would a fetus develop without a hand or leg, or other missing body part, as happened to many in the UVA study? If the soul had entered at a later time, the fetus would already have begun developing the missing body part.

Who is likely to suffer from obsession or possession? A child whose personal boundaries are weak, or even an adult, who has been weaken because of illness or an accident, may be vulnerable. Most are invaded by wandering spirits, or even relatives, who have died. Dr. Modi says possession by evil spirits, demons, or an entity identifying himself as Satan is rare but not unheard of.

A number of mental health professionals, including psychiatrists and psychologists, now treat possession, or its lesser form, obsession. Officials of the Roman Catholic Church still train a number of priests each year to conduct exorcisms, and they officially designate and specify those deemed qualified for the task. Yet, exorcism has been strictly controlled by the Church in modern times. According to one source, a 27 page ritual exists that is followed to drive out demons. Moreover, an exorcism isn't something a parish priest can decide on his own to do. Church canon requires an exorcism be performed only upon a direct order "of the bishop, after two careful investigations, based on positive indications that possession is in fact present."

The Catholic Church Continues to Perform Exorcisms

According to the memoirs of Cardinal Jacques Martin [no relation], the former prefect of the pontifical household, Pope John Paul II successfully exorcised a woman in 1982. She was brought to him writhing on the ground. Father Gabriele Amorth told *La Stampa,* an Italian newspaper, that Pope John Paul II successfully conducted three exorcisms during his pontificate. Amorth said, "He carried out these exorcisms because he wanted to give a powerful example. He wanted to give the message that we must once again start exorcising those who are possessed by demons . . . I have seen many strange things [during exorcisms] . . . objects such as nails spat out. The devil told a woman that he would make her spit out a transistor radio and lo and behold she started spitting out bits and pieces of a radio transistor. I have seen levitations, and a force that needed six or eight men to hold the person still. Such things are rare, but they happen."

Malachi Martin
(1921-1999)

An absolutely fascinating book on this subject was published by Reader's Digest Press in 1976 called *Hostage to the Devil*. It was written by Malachi Martin (1921 – 1999), also no relation, a former Jesuit Professor at the Pontifical Biblical Institute in Rome, who studied at Oxford and has a doctorate in Semitic languages, archeology, and Oriental history. The book gives extensive background about and relates the full details of five actual exorcisms conducted under the sanction of the Roman Catholic Church. Do not read this book at night if you are alone. Apparently, the depiction of an exorcism related in the popular book and movie, *The Exorcist*, is accurate because that's what the exorcisms Malachi Martin described were like. It's a gross understatement to say that Satan and his buddies are a really, really nasty bunch. You thought Jeffery Dahlmer was sick? He was a Boy Scout by comparison.

Non Religious Exorcisms

In recent years, a number of psychiatrists, psychologists, and other mental health practitioners have gotten into the business of what they call "depossession." They'd rather call it depossession than exorcism I suppose because they don't approach it from a religious perspective. They say they rarely encounter Satan and his demons although they tend to agree Satan and his minions exist, and that obsession or possession by them can happen. According Dr. Louise Ireland-Frey, a psychiatrist, "[Satan and demons] do not belong to the human kingdom, being the negative aspect, composed of the 'fallen angels' and their slaves. This is not drawn from a religious source . . . I have been told these things by the dark entities [I have] encountered. A number of them have told us that they are delighted to get us to believe that they exist only when we think of them, speak of them, and 'believe in' them—it makes their work of invading easier! On the other hand, thinking fearfully of them, brooding compulsively, talking often of them certainly does predispose a person to attracting their focused attention."

The approach used to depossess a patient who is afflicted in this way is less confrontational than that of an exorcism by a Catholic priest. In addition, the therapist routinely tries to help the invading spirit find its way into the light.

Let me pause here to say, much has already been written about this. I conducted a Google search and turned up a web site that offered a dozen different books on the subject. I'm going to relate some of what Dr. Louise Ireland-Frey has to say in her book, *Freeing the Captives: The Emerging Therapy of Spirit Attachment* (Hampton Roads, 1999) because her credentials are strong. She's a Phi Beta Kappa

graduate of Colorado University, has a master of arts degree from Mount Holyoke College in Massachusetts, and a medical degree from Tulane University.

Dr. Louise Ireland-Frey spent a full career as a medical doctor and psychiatrist before, at the age of 67, she began using hypnotism to help those who suffer past-life trauma. She also uses it to detach earthbound spirits who may be causing trouble for her patients. She says that when her clients are regressed to a previous life and come to the death experience terminating that lifetime, it's possible to continue the regression past the physical death and on into the after-death state. Similarly, when she contacts earthbound entities—those who may or may not have attached themselves to a living person—she can also ask them to recall the circumstances of their physical death. Dr. Ireland-Frey uses an intermediary to make this contact. Essentially, she hypnotizes someone, either the patient she is trying to help, or a willing assistant, and has the hypnotized individual "channel" the earth-bound entity.

Using this procedure she has learned what we already surmised from NDEs. A person's consciousness typically floats above the its body for a short time after death. The disembodied consciousness usually feels free and light and relieved, and it senses it can go wherever it seems to be drawn. At this point it might be drawn through what seems a tunnel and into the light. This light is perceived as alive and sentient, a Being of Light who welcomes the personality with understanding, kindness, and love. She says that in fact most people find themselves going to a state that is peaceful and beautiful. Only an occasional person reports a chilly, lonely, or horrifying, hell-like experience.

She has also learned through this procedure the stages after death which we've already touched on—the life review, for example, in which the activities, actions, thoughts, and words of the entire life are reviewed and evaluated as to their value and impact on others. The individual sees both his or her successes, weaknesses, and failures, and in this way judges for him or herself the worth and value of the life just past. Another stage is one Ireland-Frey calls the "cleansing" which is often described as the feeling of being embraced or surrounded by light.

It seems to me the world would be a much better place if everyone accepted this model of what happens. So many of us now believe that when they die, that's it—nothingness—and they live their lives accordingly. They think, "Might as well live it up—who cares who gets hurt in the process?"

If so, they may be sorry they didn't read this book. Experience for the sake of experience becomes their life goal, rather than achievement, service to others, and the development of character.

Young people take heed. And don't be discouraged while reading this if you are getting on in years. It's never too late to make amends—even to those who may have gone before you. Think about them. Picture them in your mind's eye, and tell them you're sorry. It certainly can't hurt, and will probably help a great deal.

And it's never too late to be learning things you can carry over to the next life. Find something you feel passionate about and pursue it. When you come back next time, you will have a head start on what may be your life's calling. Want to be a novelist? Start writing that novel. It doesn't matter if it doesn't get published this time around. You're learning to write. Knowledge is one of the few things you can take with you, remember?

How Souls Become Invaders of the Living

As we have already learned, not all souls go through the stages out-lined above. As was touched on, a person who is heavy with negative emotions and undesirable habits such as rage, cruelty, greed and so forth may be too negative to be attracted to the light, and will turn away, per-haps not even perceiving it, and go to a "place"—a vibrational frequency, or "dimension"—that is appropriate to its present nature, i.e., dark and heavy. Ireland-Frey says souls are a little like substances suspended in water, the "heaviest" after death sink to the lowest astral levels, the "lightest" float to the upper levels, and the rest find the appropriate lev-els in-between.

Many die not having a clear idea of what to expect after death and find themselves bewildered upon discovering they are still aware. It is as though they are alive, but their bodies are dead and they can't reenter them. Rather than going to the light or finding an appropriate vibra-tional level, they remain on the earth plane where they are able to see and hear living persons but are invisible and inaudible to them. These souls are likely to find this situation frustrating. Not knowing what to do or where to go, many such disembodied spirits start to wander, either aimlessly, or perhaps to some chosen place or to be near a special person.

Some wanderers remain in the area of their body—which may now be buried. I have a friend, for example, who says he is sensitive to the presence of the disembodied and will not go near a graveyard. Others may find a home in a house or other building and become the "ghosts" who haunt these places.

According to Dr. Ireland-Frey, many wanderers find a place that seems lighter or warmer than the chilly darkness of the earth-bound state in which they have been, and it turns out to be the body or aura of a living person—often without either the living host or the invading spirit being aware of the relationship.

What sort of person is a likely host for an invading spirit? As briefly noted, a person whose aura is weak or "open" is most susceptible. This may be because the individual has been in an accident, or suffered an illness, been under an anesthetic for an operation, or recently suffered an emotional shock such as grief or fear. Children, whose auras are not yet fully protective, are also vulnerable. In addition, Occult activities such working a Ouija board may open an invasion path.

Five Degrees of Spirit Attachment

Several degrees of closeness of such attachments have been identified by Dr. Ireland-Frey as well as other therapists in her line of work. The first level is that of temptation of the living person by an aspect of the wanderer. This is not really an overwhelming compulsion but the thought or idea of doing or saying something that is contrary to the basic personality of the living individual—something out of character.

The second level is called "influencing" or "shadowing." In this instance, the disembodied entity is affecting the host person mildly or intermittently, as with mood swings, irrational moments, sudden inexplicable fears or depressions.

Third, in situations where the entity is affecting the host's personal feelings and habits more noticeably and frequently, the word "oppression" or "harassing" is used. Dr. Ireland-Frey says someone who is clairvoyant may be able to see the entity attached to the host's aura or within it.

Obsession is the fourth step up. Here Dr. Ireland-Frey's definition differs slightly from that of the Roman Catholic Church. She says it's a remarkably common condition in which the entity may invade not only the psyche but also the physical body of the host and meld its own personality traits and former bodily feelings with those of the host, often to the confusion and bewilderment of that person. The affected person may become aware of persistent pains, sudden changes in emotions unlike his or her normal feelings, unfamiliar attitudes, or even unnatural traits and talents.

And finally, number five is "possession," the condition wherein the invading entity takes over the body of the host completely, pushing out the host's soul and expressing its own words, feelings, and behaviors through the host's body. Dr. Ireland-Frey says complete possession is rare, and can be spectacular when it happens. Sometimes it may alternate with obsession. A case when a person suddenly goes berserk, for example, may be the result of sudden, complete possession. She writes that she has personally seen only one case of complete possession.

Monroe's Research Supports Aspects of Ireland-Frey's

Dr. Ireland-Frey's observations dovetail in many respects with the findings of Robert Monroe, founder of The Monore Institute. In addition to souls stuck on earth, Monroe found there to be bands of energy around the planet where people are stuck. In at least one of these, he found souls caught up in hedonistic pursuits where they were mindlessly pursuing orgiastic sexual activity. He also found that physical sites exist on the planet where people are caught up as well. As a result, he devoted a good deal of his time and energy to helping people move from these sites to what he called "The Reception Center"—the realm of light at the end of the tunnel. While in the out-of-body state, Monroe was able to see these discarnates, and they were able to see him. He was able to explain to them that they were stuck and was able to coax them along.

The Lifeline Program

Monroe and his staff at The Monroe Institute actually developed a protocol for helping lost or stuck souls find their way and, as I understand it, this is still put to use today following major disasters that suddenly take the lives of many people. Called the Liveline Program, it was set up to rescue souls who are lost or stuck. Often, a soul will be in denial and keep repeating whatever activity the person was involved in before death. Since time does not exist in the spiritual realm, this can go on indefinitely.

Rescuing of Souls after Terrorist Attacks

Groups of graduates of the Monroe Institute teamed up after the Oklahoma City bombings, and again after the 911, attacks to help free stuck souls, following those disasters. A total of 168 persons were killed in Oklahoma City. Apparently more than half were stuck. It's not surprising many did not know they had died since the bombing came without warning. The attack on the Twin Towers caused many more deaths, but only a small percentage became stuck. Most were not killed instantly. They knew they were going to die. Although they went through a horrifying experience, most passed into the light soon after death. To me, this is preferable to becoming stuck in place and time.

It must have been a big job freeing so many stuck souls, but the out-of-body rescuers were able to confront them, explain the situation and lead them to the light. As they approached the reception center—the realm of light—beings of light came forward, took over from the rescuers and helped the newly-deceased transition to their new surroundings.

You may be wondering why the beings of light didn't go down to the physical plane to help those stuck. Because of different frequencies in the various realms or levels of the spirit world, most beings who reside in the realm of light and higher are unable to descent to the earth plane. Thus, the out-of-body explorers performed an important service that may otherwise never have taken place.

OBE Explorers Can Go into the Light

While beings of light cannot descend to earth, at least some OBE adepts are able to proceed into the realm of light and actually meet with friends and relatives who have passed on. Robert Monroe himself, who died in 1995, has been visited on occasion by prior students and living friends.

One might wonder what people do to amuse themselves while they are dead, or between lives, and residing in the realm of light or some higher level of non physical reality. The answer is, "Whatever they want."

In that realm, our thoughts instantly create our reality and environment. Robert Monroe, who was perhaps the most accomplished and extensively traveled out-of-body adept said that in the early stages following a normal death, souls may recreate the living environment they have just left. Monroe visited a deceased neighbor of his, a physician in life, and found him working in a garden identical to the one located behind his home in the life just concluded. References to this sort of thing can be found in ancient literature such as the *Tibetan Book of the Dead*.

A soul often processes the life just past by recreating various aspects of it during what might be called a period of assimilation. This is what many of the University of Virginia subjects skipped. Over time—a paradox because there is no time—the personality of the former life becomes incorporated into the soul, after which it may or may not choose to incarnate once again.

I'm willing to bet, however, most souls incarnate many times. Next, we will look at one way many believe soul evolution, through multiple incarnations, may actually work.

Chapter Seven
The Cosmology of Soul Evolution

Concerning human evolution through reincarnation, one school of thought has to do with Michael cosmology. Michael is an arbitrary name given to what some believe to be an entity comprised of about 1050 human souls that exists on a higher plane of consciousness than those of us here in physical reality. Michael is thought to communicate with incarnate earthlings through a dozen or so channels or mediums. A number of books have been written by them. The first was published in 1979, written by Chelsea Quinn Yarbro, called *Messages from Michael on the Nature of the Evolution of the Human Soul.* To get an indication of how widely known the Michael cosmology has become, I plugged the words "Michael Teachings" into Google. A total of 62.5 million hits turned up. I'd say that's pretty widespread.

According to Michael via his channels, the human population on earth is made up of five different soul age categories: Infant, Baby, Young, Mature, and Old. Within each soul age are seven steps or stages, making 35 stages (5 x 7 = 35) in all that are passed through before a soul stops incarnating.

Each step or stage takes one or more lifetimes to complete. I have been told that on average about 110 to 120 lifetimes are required for a soul to pass through all 35. Some souls take many more, some less, but even so, a soul's journey is not finished once it stops incarnating. A number of non physical planes are said to exist that must also be traversed on a soul's journey back to the godhead, or Tao, as Michael refers to

God—the ground of being or Universal Mind that gives rise to all that is. Once reunited with the godhead, a soul may decide to go back to square one and begin the long journey—called a "grand cycle"—once again. According to a Michael reading I had done on myself in preparation for an interview with well-known Michael channel Shepherd Hoodwin, I am on my ninth grand cycle, and my soul age this time through is the seventh level of the mature stage (see the chart he prepared for me on the page opposite). If this is true, I calculate I've got about 21 and probably more lifetimes to go before I stop incarnating.

Wears me out to think about it.

The Michael cosmology may or may not be the way things really are, but I have a friend I've known for more than twenty years—a successful and intelligent guy whom I trust—who tells me he's in touch on a regular basis with both Michael and another group soul entity on an even higher plane. He has given the name Group Seven to this even higher plane entity. He says Group Seven confirms the Michael cosmology in principle if not in every specific detail.

A Sixteen Year Old's Guides Explain Life

The same friend had an extraordinary experience at the age of 16, which says a lot about our existence as human souls who have incarnated here on earth. This man is now 64 years old and the head of the sizable law firm. As a successful lawyer who knows some of his clients and potential clients will think he belongs in the loony bin after they read this story, he asked me not to use his real name. So I'll call him Thomas—a name he says he once had in a prior life.

MICHAEL READING

NAME   Stephen Hawley Martin

By Shepherd Hoodwin (949) 429-8792 877-SUMMERJoy
99 Pearl Laguna Niguel CA 92677-4818
sgh@summerjoy.com
http://summerjoy.com

REQUESTED BY   12/21/2008

ESSENCE

	INSPIRATION		EXPRESSION		ACTION		ASSIMILATION
	Ordinal	Cardinal	Ordinal	Cardinal	Ordinal	Cardinal	Neutral
ROLE	○ SERVER	○ PRIEST	○ ARTISAN	○ SAGE	○ WARRIOR	○ KING	◉ SCHOLAR
	+ Knowledge, – Theory						
ESSENCE TWIN	○ Server	○ Priest	○ Artisan	○ Sage	○ Warrior	○ King	◉ Scholar
	Discarnate						

CADENCE POSITION   5 + Expansion, – Adventure   **CADENCE** 1   **GREATER CADENCE** 1

Position Resonates W/	○ Server (1)	○ Priest (6)	○ Artisan (2)	◉ Sage (5)	○ Warrior (3)	○ King (7)	○ Scholar (4)

CADRE/ENTITY   8 / 3   Love Side

TASK COMPANION(S)   Warrior, discarnate.

MALE/FEMALE ENERGY   31/69

FREQUENCY 47

PREVIOUS CYCLES   8

OVERLEAVES

NEEDS   Acceptance   Adventure   Freedom

LIFE QUADRANT   ○ LOVE ◉ KNOWLEDGE ○ POWER ○ SUPPORT

	INSPIRATION		EXPRESSION		ACTION		ASSIMILATION
	Ordinal	Cardinal	Ordinal	Cardinal	Ordinal	Cardinal	Neutral
GOAL	○ REEVALUATION	○ GROWTH	○ DISCRIMINATION	○ ACCEPTANCE	○ SUBMISSION	○ DOMINANCE	◉ FLOW
	+ Suspension, – Inertia						
ATTITUDE	○ STOIC	○ SPIRITUALIST	○ SKEPTIC	○ IDEALIST	○ CYNIC	◉ REALIST	○ PRAGMATIST
	+ Perception, – Supposition						
MODE	○ RESERVE	○ PASSION	○ CAUTION	○ POWER	○ PERSEVERANCE	○ AGGRESSION	◉ OBSERVATION
	+ Clarity, – Surveillance						
CENTER	○ EMOTIONAL		◉ INTELLECTUAL		○ PHYSICAL	○ MOVING	
	+ Thought, – Reason		Moving Part				
CHIEF OBSTACLE	○ SELF-DEPRECATION	◉ ARROGANCE	○ SELF-DESTRUCTION	○ GREED	○ MARTYRDOM	○ IMPATIENCE	○ STUBBORNNESS
	+ Pride, – Vanity						
BODY TYPE	○ LUNAR	○ SATURNIAN	○ JOVIAL	○ MERCURIAL	○ VENUSIAN	◉ MARTIAL	○ SOLAR
	+ Wiry, – Muscle-bound		Secondary(ies) Lunar				

SOUL AGE   ○ INFANT ○ BABY ○ YOUNG ◉ MATURE ○ OLD   ○ 1 ○ 2 ○ 3 ○ 4 ○ 5 ○ 6 ◉ 7   **MANIFESTING**   Mature 5

Thomas did not have an easy childhood. His mother was a paranoid schizophrenic. He knew this, including the terminology, because his father was a psychiatrist. Who knows . . . maybe the dad married Thomas' mom because he thought he could cure her if he devoted enough time and energy to the project, and really worked at it.

He was wrong.

The result was Thomas never knew how his mother was going to react. His life was in constant turmoil. On top of this, he had fallen in love with his best friend's girlfriend and the girlfriend had given him indications she felt the same toward him. Of course, he did not want to hurt his friend, but at the age of 16 those infamous male hormones were raging and he was upset and confused.

The night the visit with his guides took place, his best friend was spending the night with him, in his bedroom, in a twin bed just a few feet away. It was 3:30 a.m.; his friend was fast asleep. Thomas was wide awake—wondering what to do, and wishing fervently he'd never been born. Then he wouldn't have all these problems to deal with.

Suddenly, a tornado-like vortex swooped down from above and yanked his consciousness out of his body. It seemed to catapult him up through the roof of his house in a arch like a Fourth of July rocket.

Within seconds Thomas found himself high above the earth looking down. He could see the whole of its curvature. The outline of the east coast was apparent because of the twinkling lights of the cities. He could look out over the Atlantic and see the demarcation of dark and light as dawn approached. Looking up, the firmament of the sky was nothing less than spectacular—thousands or perhaps millions of stars sparkling above.

"While I was on the way up," Thomas told me, "I didn't have time to wonder if this was a dangerous situation I was in. But that thought did cross my mind once the movement stopped."

"But you didn't have a body," I said.

"Exactly—that was my immediate response as well. I didn't know how I'd gotten there, or even what part of me was actually there, but I didn't have a body—so what was there to worry about?"

Thomas said he could see without eyes, was fully present and aware and was wondering how this could be, when he heard a barely audible pop.

"It resembled the slight pop one might hear if one is in a silent room and a bubble travels up through the neck of a long neck beer bottle and out the top. This carried with it the sense it was coming from the top of my head—the head I didn't have.

"When this occurred, the earth disappeared. The sky disappeared. The stars—everything was gone. In the place I associated with my location was a faint glimmer of flickering light, a sort of dotted outline, which I took to be some sort of consciousness or spiritual essence."

Thomas says he thought if this flickering light represented him, then perhaps there were others in this space.

"Then I saw—in what seemed the distance—other flickers of light. Many of them. I wondered if they might also be discarnate beings, so I asked the question, 'Is any body there?'

"As far as I was concerned, I vocalized this, but of course I had no vocal cords because I had no body."

I asked Thomas, "Did any one answer?"

"An answer came immediately. It was, 'Yes.' And these string-like flickering light beings moved toward me and surrounded me. I'm not sure how many there were but I would say about three dozen.

"In the dialog that ensued they all seemed to talk with a single voice—sort of like surround sound, or you might say, quadraphonic."

"Then what happened?" I asked.

"A dialog—I asked them a number of questions and they answered."

"This is fascinating," I said. "Tell me, what did you ask them?"

"My first question was, 'Where am I?'"

"And?"

"Not long after all this happened, I made copious notes and eventually wrote them up, so I can tell you exactly what they said. They said, 'You are in a place that is no place.'

"'What does that mean?' I said, and they said, 'You are outside of space and time as you know it.'

"'What am I doing here?'

"They said, 'We brought you here because we have some very important things to tell you.'

"'Oh, okay,' I said. 'Who are you?'

"'We are your guides.'

"This was in 1960, and I was 16 years old. I knew nothing about such things. I had no idea what they were talking about. So I said, 'What are guides?'

"They said, 'You can think of us as that which is both you and not you.'

"'Me and not me?'"

I couldn't help breaking in and said, "Sounds like, 'What is the sound of one hand clapping?'"

"Exactly," Thomas said. "So then I said that if you're not going to tell me what guides are, can you at least tell me what guides do?

"And they went on to give a beautiful and quite comforting explanation. They said everyone—all living people—have guides. Guides are souls who sign on to facilitate the development of those of us who are embodied."

I said, "Did they give you any advice about your current situation?

About your dilemma concerning your friend and his girlfriend and wishing you had never been born?"

"They did," Thomas said. "After we got through the explanation of who they were, I asked them what important message they had brought me here to tell.

"They said, 'The message is, your life is your own. It belongs to you.'

"I said, 'Who else would it belong to?'

"They said, 'We mean, you are free to do anything you want with your life, or to do nothing with it at all. You can be whatever you want, you can do whatever you want, you can say whatever you want, you can think and feel whatever you want, and whatever you do or don't do with it is perfectly okay.'

"And they went on to say, and this was the heart of the matter, 'Even if you should decide to self destruct'—they didn't use the term, suicide—'even if you should decide to terminate your life because it's unpleasant, or for whatever reason, that's perfectly okay. You may have been taught in school, or in church, that it's not okay, that it's some kind of a sin, that you will go to hell, or whatever—forget all that. It's simply not true. None of that is the way things really are—"

I couldn't help myself, and broke in again, "But there must be some consequences—"

Thomas said, "Oh, they didn't say there wouldn't be consequences. At this point, I started getting on the defensive. I saw where they were going and told them to wait a minute—I hadn't been planning to self destruct—or kill myself, or anything like that.

"And they said, 'You had not reached that point yet. But if the thoughts you were having of wishing you did not exist had been followed to their conclusion—if we had not intervened—you would have reached that point. And in some other situations, you may reach that point. And we are here to tell you, that's okay. You won't be judged.

"And then they delivered the punch line. They said, 'But we want you to know that choice would be a waste of time.'"

I said, "Well, how does that work? What happens? Do you have to come back and do it all over again?"

Thomas said, "Exactly—let me tell you. As a 16 year old, when they threw out the words 'waste of time,' that was something I could appreciate. I said, 'Waste of time? What does that mean?'

"They answered by giving me an explanation of the way life and evolution work. In summary, they said we go through a potentially infinite number of lifetimes and for the most part we choose our lifetimes, and what we're likely to experience in each. The thing that had been completely erroneous in my thinking and outlook before they brought me to that place was the idea I could cease to exist.

"'You can terminate a lifetime,' they said, 'but you cannot cease to exist. There is only life. If you decide to exit the one you are in you will simply have to come back and face the same situations again until you deal with and get through them. That's the way it is. Once you have started on a curriculum, you have to see it through."

I said, "That reminds me of the movie, *Groundhog Day*. The main character gets stuck living the same day over and over again, until he gets it right. Only then does he finally move on."

"A perfect allegory for the human condition," Thomas said.

I asked Thomas why he thought his guides had intervened, that plenty of people commit suicide, and their guides don't stop them.

He told me it was because he had committed suicide in other lives and had a tendency to do so. For this reason, they had been quick to act.

I guess they were tired of him wasting time.

By the way, Thomas was sent back to his body and slept soundly for what was left of the night. And in case you're wondering, he did not pursue his best friend's girlfriend. Two days following his extraordinary meeting with his guides—after he had started a job as a lifeguard for the summer—he met a girl and fell head over heels. His best friend's girlfriend was quickly—and completely—forgotten.

Chapter Eight
The Science of Reincarnation

According to Dr. Tucker, for individual cases he and his colleagues have studied, it is possible to come up with arguments that cast doubt on reincarnation as the cause, but reincarnation is the only viable explanation to explain all the UVA cases when viewed as a whole. Julie Beischel will no doubt go ahead with her research to find out if psychics are using the psychic reservoir, ESP or superpsi to give information about discarnates. What she learns will surely be interesting. But it seems to me the continuation of consciousness of specific individuals has been clearly demonstrated by Ian Stevenson's and Jim Tucker's research. A psychic reservoir, ESP or superpsi, can in no way explain what often accompanies children's memories of past lives—birthmarks that mimic the wounds that ended the past life, the strong emotion many of the children feel about their past life and the loved ones they left behind. It cannot explain food preferences, sexual orientation, phobias, and cravings on the part of some for alcohol or tobacco. If want to know more about this, I recommend Dr. Tucker's book, *Life Before Life*.

The Mind Can Exist Separated from the Body

That reincarnation is a fact is going to be difficult for some to swallow. It clearly indicates that our mind or soul—what Stevenson called the "reincarnating personality"—must be able to exist independently of the brain and body in some sort of mental space or discarnate realm.

The data base at the University of Virginia indicates that about one in five children reporting past life memories also report memories of the time spent between the past life and this one. Stevenson theorized there might be an intermediate vehicle, made of "nonmaterial mind stuff" that imprints the embryo or fetus with memories of injuries or other markings of the previous body, together with likes, dislikes, and other attitudes.

Rupert Sheldrake

Rupert Sheldrake, a British biochemist, graduate of Cambridge University and former Royal Society research fellow, has set forth a hypothesis that explains this. According to Sheldrake, the growth, development and the programmed behavior of organisms are governed by fields which exist much like fields of gravity or electromagnetism, and that these fields change and evolve as a species changes and evolves. Each plant, animal and human has its own field which is part of a larger field of its species just as a radio show has its own particular frequency but is nonetheless part of the full band of radio frequencies on the AM or FM radio dial.

Sheldrake is not the only one to have come up with such a theory. A man named Harold S. Burr, Ph.D., (1889-1973) did also. Dr. Burr was E. K. Hunt Professor Emeritus, Anatomy, at Yale University School of Medicine and a member of the faculty of medicine for more than forty years. From 1916 to the late 1950's, he published, either alone or with others, more than ninety-three scientific papers. Dr. Burr maintained that all living things—from men to mice, from trees to seeds—are molded and controlled by electro-dynamic fields, which he was able to measure and map with standard voltmeters. He maintained that these "fields of life," or L-fields as he called them, are the basic blueprints of all life.

Morphogenetic Fields Work Together with Our Genes

Sheldrake's theory is essentially the same. According to him, genes and morphogenetic fields work together to create our bodies. Genes account for such things as hair and eye color, and other inherited features. Morphogenetic fields guide the cells of a growing fetus to become a kidney or a foot or a brain while an animal or human embryo is forming in the womb.

Traditional biology assumes genes are programmed with the purpose of each new cell and direct it to form whatever body part it is assigned to, but this has never been demonstrated. Sheldrake says genes dictate the primary structure of proteins, not the individual parts of the body. According to currently accepted theory, given the right genes and hence the right proteins, and the right systems by which protein synthesis is controlled, an organism is supposed to assemble itself. But how does this actually work? As Rupert Sheldrake once wrote, "This is rather like delivering the right materials to a building site at the right times and expecting a house to grow spontaneously."

Physiologists do their best to explain the functioning of plants and animals in mechanistic terms, but explanations of some phenomena are sketchy at best. Sheldrake believes the following can be explained by the existence of morphogenetic fields: Formation of the structure of organisms, instinctive behavior, learning, and memory.

Sheldrake's theory also clears up certain mysteries that currently remain with respect to the theory of evolution. According to the fossil record, a species can remain virtually unchanged for many millennia and then alter dramatically during an epoch when environmental conditions shift. This happens so quickly that scientists often are unable to find evidence of the transition. An eminent authority on evolution, Stephen Jay Gould (1941 – 2002), once wrote, "The extreme rarity of transitional forms in the fossil record persists as the trade secret of paleontology. The evolutionary trees that adorn our textbooks have data only at the tips and nodes of their branches; the rest is inference, however reasonable, not the evidence of fossils."

One Way Evolution Might Work

It seems a reasonable possibility we humans and everything else in the universe evolved out of an organizing intelligence that at this point I shall call spirit. In the beginning, spirit created an almost infinite number of variations of living things. Let's say they were one celled animals in the sea. Those that were most suited to the environment survived. They reproduced by the millions, each offspring slightly different from its siblings. More complicated forms were the result. Again, those best suited to the environment survived and reproduced. And so on and so on.

As evolution progressed, living organisms themselves developed intelligence. This intelligence impressed itself upon the organizing intelligence of spirit, and the organizing intelligence of spirit went to work to create ever more sophisticated and evolved adaptations. The result of this process can be seen in ever-increasing levels of intelligence displayed by ever more evolved life forms. As intelligence evolves it becomes and more more self aware.

Let's say there are now animals walking around on land that are at least somewhat self aware. One such animal eats leaves and lives in an environment that's changing from forest to savanna. Plenty of leaves were available to eat in the forest. But dryer conditions are developing, punctuated by rainy spells, and much of the low lying vegetation has died off and been replaced by grass. Some trees are able to survive the dry spells, and more and more, the leaves that remain in this changing environment are found on trees that tend to be fairly high off the ground.

Perhaps this animal walks each day by trees the leaves of which are too high for him to reach. He thinks to himself, "Doggone it, if only I had a longer neck I could feast on those leaves up there." In some way or other this remedy to the predicament forms in the animal's subconscious mind, which is an aspect of the species' mophogenetic field. Newborns of this species begin being born with longer necks as a result, and the animal we know as a giraffe develops in a short period of time. Natural selection also favors those with longer necks and works together with the morphogenetic field in a push-me pull-me effect.

Tasmanian Devils Show Rapid Evolution

A recent example may be that of the Tasmanian devil, reported on in a July 15, 2008, *Associated Press* article. The case was written up by researchers at the University of Tasmania in Australia. Faced with an epidemic of cancer that cuts their lives short, Tasmanian devils have begun breeding at much younger ages than one would expect.

"We could be seeing evolution occurring before our eyes. Watch this space!" zoologist Menna Jones of the university was quoted as having said.

Tasmanian devils live on the island of Tasmania, south of Australia. They weigh 20 to 30 pounds and were named devils by early European settlers because the furry black marsupials produce a fierce screech and can be bad-tempered.

Since 1996 a contagious form of cancer called devil facial tumor disease has been infecting these animals and is invariably fatal, causing death between the ages of two and three.

Tasmanian Devil

In the past devils would live five to six years, breeding at ages two, three and four, but with the new disease, even females who breed at two may not live long enough to rear their first litter.

Jones, who has been studying the animals' life cycles since before the disease outbreak, noted that there has been a 16-fold increase in breeding at age one. She reported her findings in the July 14, 2008 edition of *Proceedings of the National Academy of Sciences.*

The disease could cause the devils to become extinct in 25 years or so, she said, but this change to younger breeding may slow population decline and reduce the chance of them disappearing.

The Panda's Thumb

If you've ever been to the National Zoo in Washington, you've probably watched the giant pandas eating bamboo leaves. They take stalk after stalk and slide them between thumb and forefinger, stripping them, then popping this mouthwatering high-fiber food in their mouths. You may have wondered how these big guys got thumbs since primates are the ones with opposing digits. Pandas belong to the family Procyonidae (raccoons, kinkajous, et cetera) of the order Carnivora, one of the hallmarks of which is that all five digits on the front paw point forward and have claws for ripping flesh.

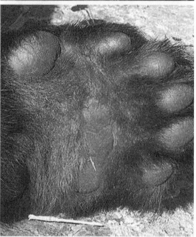

The Panda's Thumb Is Not a Thumb at All

On close inspection you'll find that the panda's thumb is not a thumb at all but a "complex structure formed by marked enlargement of a (wrist) bone and an extensive rearrangement of musculature." Not having the thumb needed to make bamboo eating easy, the panda took what he had to work with and evolved one of a makeshift variety, according to biologist Stephen Jay Gould, who also wrote, "The panda's thumb provides an elegant zoological counterpart to Darwin's orchids. An engineer's best solution is debarred by history. The panda's true thumb is committed to another role, too specialized for a different function to become an opposable, manipulating digit. So the panda must use parts on hand and settle for an enlarged wrist bone and a somewhat clumsy, but quite workable, solution." Gould added, "Odd arrangements and funny solutions are the proof of evolution—paths that a sensible God would never tread but that a natural process, constrained by history, follows perforce."*

Where Memories Reside

Morphogenetic fields also explain a phenomenon of memory which has neuroscientists puzzled: where it is located in the brain. One way research on this subject has been conducted is to train an animal to do something and then to cut out parts of its brain in an effort to find where the memory was stored. As Sheldrake has written, "But even after large chunks of their brains have been removed—in some experiments over 60 percent—the hapless animals can often remember what they were trained to do before the operation."

Several theories have been put forth to explain this including backup systems and holograms, but the obvious one in light of Sheldrake's hypothesis is that the memory may not be in the brain at all. This has been proven by the past-life research conducted by the University of Virginia in that subjects report memories from between lives when they have no physical body or brain. I asked Dr. Tucker about this. He said brains are needed to recall memories, but it appears brains are not where memories are stored.

---

* Gould, Stephen Jay, *The Panda's Thumb,* W.W. Norton & Company, New York, 1980, pages 20-24.

The bottom line is, scientists have been looking in the wrong place. To quote Sheldrake again, "A search inside your TV set for traces of the programs you watched last week would be doomed to failure for the same reason: The set tunes in to TV transmissions but does not store them." In other words, the brain is a physical link to the memory located either in our morphogenetic field, or perhaps in our own little cubby in the psychic reservoir.

Instincts May Be Memories Housed in Morphogenetic Fields

It seems logical to me the morphogenetic fields of individual humans blend into the overall morphogenetic field of humankind. Each one affects the whole in terms of where the species stands in evolution. The same is true of species of animals. This has obvious implications in the explanation of instinctive behavior. The collective field of a species that is hunted—deer, for example—learns over time to be afraid of man. An individual deer does not have to learn this after birth. He is born with it, and we label it "instinctive behavior." It's part of the collective memory of deer which is contained in the morphogenetic field of the species.

Adherents to the "survival of the fittest" theory will argue that of the many deer that are born each spring, those that possess a natural inclination to skittishness are more likely to reach the age of reproduction, and this is what has caused the trait to develop into an instinct over time. This makes sense as well, so it's hard to argue. My guess is—since most things have more than one cause—that both theories are correct and in fact work together as written above in the hypothetical case of the evolution of giraffes.

Other Evidence of Morphogenetic Fields

The fact of a collective morphogenetic field helps explain the behavior of societal insects, fishes and birds. For example, we've all seen swarms of gnats, schools of fish, or flocks of birds behaving as though they were a single organism  as they glide through the air or water, turning and diving as though they form one unified whole. Spend some time at an aquarium watching a school of fish. Something is sure to cause a minor explosion in their midst, producing momentary chaos as individuals scatter a short distance from their original positions. But within seconds, they will regroup and become a single moving organism once more.

The behavior of some species is truly amazing, or would be without Sheldrake's and Dr. Burr's theory. Key West silver-sided fish, for example, will organize themselves around a barracuda in a shape that seems dictated by risk. The distance between the school and the barracuda is widest at the predator's mouth and narrowest at the tail, where the threat of being eaten is the least.

In the world of insects, African termites, which are blind, rebuild tunnels and arches from both sides of a breach and meet up perfectly in the middle, and they can do this even when the two sides are separated by a large steel plate that is several feet wider and higher than the termitary, placed so that it divides the mound.

Acquired Characteristics Can Be Passed Along

Be all this as it may, what may be mind-blowing about Sheldrake's hypothesis to those accustomed to thinking of heredity as working solely by the passing of genes through egg and sperm is this: acquired characteristics can be passed from one generation to the next. As we know, Dr. Stevenson found that birthmarks and other physiological manifestations often relate to experiences of the remembered past life, particularly when violent death was involved. In my interview with Dr. Tucker, he pointed out that in some situations mental images are known to produce specific effects on the body. For example, some religiously devout individuals develop wounds, called stigmata, that match the crucifixion wounds of Jesus. More than 350 such cases have been reported.

Someone under hypnosis might be told a pencil is a lit cigarette. When that person's arm is touched by the pencil, a cigarette burn will appear on the arm.

In another case, Dr. Tucker said a man who remembered a traumatic event when he was tied up developed rope marks on his arms. It's amazing what belief and the power of the mind can create.

Let's take a look at the awesome power of belief.

The Power of Belief

The effectiveness of placebos, for example, has been demonstrated time and again in double-blind scientific tests. The placebo effect—the phenomenon of patients feeling better after taking dud pills—is seen throughout the field of medicine. One report says that after thousands of studies, hundreds of millions of prescriptions and tens of billions of dollars in sales, sugar pills are as effective at treating depression as antidepressants such as Prozac, Paxil and Zoloft. What's more, placebos cause profound changes in the same areas of the brain affected by these medicines, according to this research. Thoughts and beliefs can and do produce physical changes—in this case in our bodies.

The same research reports that placebos often outperform the medicines they're up against. For example, in a trial conducted in April, 2002, comparing the herbal remedy St. John's wort to Zoloft, St. John's wort fully cured 24 percent of the depressed people who received it. Zoloft cured 25 percent. But the placebo fully cured 32 percent.

Taking what one believes to be real medicine sets up the expectation of results, and what a person expects to happen usually does happen. It's been confirmed, for example, that in cultures where belief exists in voodoo or magic, people will actually die after being cursed by a shaman. It appears such a curse has no power on an outsider who doesn't believe. The expectation causes the result. If you've read my novel, *IN MY FATHER'S HOUSE,* you know I used this phenomenon as a factor in the plot. In my book, *A Witch in the Family,* I cited this phenomenon as part of what was behind the Salem witch hysteria of

1692. I believe many of the afflicted really did believe they were being tormented by witches. Some developed lesions on their skin that looked like teeth marks where they thought witches had bitten them. Others had fits and coughed up blood.

No Wonder Athletes Get Better and Better

The implications of Sheldrake's hypothesis are incredibly widespread. To give an inkling of those falling outside the parameters of this book, consider this: during the past century athletes achieved ever higher levels of excellence in everything from Olympic track and field to tennis. Improvements in diet, equipment, training techniques and coaching have certainly played a big role, but we must now also consider whether memories located in morphogenetic fields may also be a factor. According to the theory, what has been learned by the pioneers

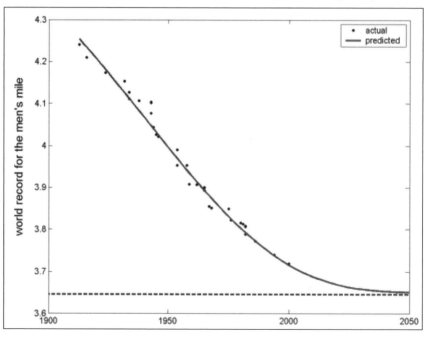

in a sport would become embedded in the morphogenetic field of humanity, and this should make learning the sport, as well as body and muscle coordination, easier for future participants. This might also account for child prodigies and virtuosos. Could it be, for example, that Tiger Woods is the incarnation of a twentieth century golfing great?

I did not begin when I was born, nor when I was conceived.
I have been growing, developing, through incalculable myriads
of millenniums . . . All my previous selves have their voices,
echoes, promptings in me . . .
Oh, incalculable times again shall I be born.

Jack London
(1876 – 1916)

Chapter Nine
A Theory to Explain How Non Physical Reality Forms the Physical

Thomas Troward (1847-1916)

A non physical reality is behind and gives rise to the physical world, just as our souls or morphogenetic fields give rise to us. But how does this work?

What I believe to be a plausible indication was given in lectures I came across given by a man named Thomas Troward. He first delivered them at Edinburgh University in Scotland in 1904. Called *The Edinburgh Lectures on Mental Science,* they provide a rationale for how mental images might account for the birthmarks as well as where we exist between lives.

Troward was born in Punjab, India, in 1847 of British parents and went to college in England, but lived most of his life in India. He was a student of metaphysics. He wrote and spoke in a kind of jargon used by nineteenth century scientists. If you have ever tried to read *The Origin of Species,* for example, you know what I mean. So I translated his lectures into plain, modern English and published them in a book called *How to Master Life* (Oaklea Press, 2007).

Troward believed that underlying everything, the ground of being of all that is, was mind—the medium of thought—and that this is what we experience and see in other living beings and living matter, such as plants and animals, as the life force.

The Phenomenon of Grace

We will explore Troward's theory, but first it is important to understand what I believe is an aspect of the life force. Though not yet recognized by established science, the life force is the direct opposite of entropy—the invisible force that causes things to break down and deteriorate. As such, the life force not only animates the body, it pushes toward growth and evolution as well health and balance in a living organism. Another word for this is grace.

Amazing Grace

Amazing Grace, how sweet the sound,
That saved a wretch like me.
I once was lost but now am found,
Was blind, but now I see.

T'was Grace that taught my heart to fear.
And Grace, my fears relieved.
How precious did that Grace appear
The hour I first believed.

Through many dangers, toils and snares
I have already come;
'Tis Grace that brought me safe thus far
and Grace will lead me home.

The Lord has promised good to me.
His word my hope secures.
He will my shield and portion be,
As long as life endures.

Yea, when this flesh and heart shall fail,
And mortal life shall cease,
I shall possess within the veil,
A life of joy and peace.

When we've been here ten thousand years
Bright shining as the sun.
We've no less days to sing God's praise
Than when we've first begun.

Grace is what happens when the life force or Universal Mind is working in people's lives to insure their growth and development. To the untrained eye, grace appears to be a set of mysterious or unexplainable conditions, events and phenomena that support, nurture, protect or enhance human life and spiritual growth. Grace works in all sorts of ways. The forms of grace seem to be universal. Our immune systems, for example, are tied to it. Modern medicine has only a vague idea why one person exposed to an infectious disease will come down with that disease and another experiencing the same level of exposure will not. On any given day, in practically every public environment, potentially lethal microbes and viruses on surfaces or floating in the air are too numerous to estimate. Yet, most people do not get sick. Why? Doctors would say it is because most people's resistance is fairly high. But what do they really mean? That most people are not rundown or depressed? Perhaps. But not everyone who is rundown and depressed contracts an infectious disease. Yet many do who are perfectly healthy and in good shape. Perhaps those in this category needed a wake up call about something going on in their lives that has them off course—a crises to jog them into reexamining the direction they are headed.

Grace Manifests in Many Ways

The grace of resistance is not limited to infectious disease. Have a chat with a state trooper who has been on the scene of a number of motor vehicle accidents. Ask him what percentage of crashes appeared fatal when he first arrived, and how many actually turned out to be. You're likely to hear some amazing stories of cars or trucks smashed beyond recognition, metal so collapsed, twisted or squashed the trooper will say, "I don't see how anyone could have survived. And yet the person walked away without a scratch," or with only minor injuries. How is it scientifically possible for metal to collapse in such a way as to conform perfectly to the shape of the human body contained inside? Nevertheless, I'm willing to bet the trooper will tell you that this happens more often than not.

When she was about a year old, my now fifteen-year-old daughter bodysurfed down the steep flight of stairs from our kitchen to our basement playroom—not just once, but twice. Another time, a baby sitter turned her back while changing a diaper, and the same daughter rolled off the counter top and fell straight to the bare kitchen floor. Any of these three falls easily could have been fatal. None caused so much as a bruise.

Almost everyone has experienced a close call that could have killed him. One day when I was fourteen, I darted across Jefferson Davis Highway without looking properly. At the time, this was the main north-south highway on the East Coast. This particular stretch had six lanes (three north and three south) with a grass median. A car struck me in mid-stride. Maybe it was the way the car's bumper caught my foot that lifted me into the air, but I should have been pushed down and run over. Instead, I was lifted up, seemed to fly through the air, and landed on the grass median. The driver was certain I was dead—until I stood up and dusted myself off. I didn't have a scratch. The only evidence of the accident was the stain on my trousers where I'd slid on the grass as I came to a stop. Also, both my shoes were missing. I found them eighty or a hundred feet away where the car had screeched to a halt. If the laws of Newtonian physics had been working that day, I wouldn't be here to put this down on paper.

How, physically, was I lifted into the air? Were angels responsible? I cannot say. But whatever happened, the phenomenon called grace came to my aid, and I lived to be an adult. As a result, I grew and studied and learned enough to enable me to write this book.

Grace Even Uses the IRS

Let me give another example. A few years ago, a friend in one of my Bible study groups and his wife quit their full time jobs in order to attend seminary together. They both had to work part-time and even then were only able to bring in enough to just get by. Unexpected bills arrived, as they always do. They totaled $578, money they simply didn't have. The couple's bank balance registered zero. They had no place to turn. Creditors were calling. Our group prayed that the money they needed would come to them. My friend and his wife prayed, too, as did others.

Two days later, the couple received an envelope in the mail from the IRS saying that their petition had been reviewed. Their tax return from two years prior had been found to be in error. Along with this notice, was a check to them for $588.

Good timing? True. But the amazing thing was, the couple had not filed a petition. Nor had they filed an amended return. Somehow or other, the IRS had done this recalculation on its own. The couple rummaged in their files and pulled out their return from two years prior. The IRS was correct. They found the error which had been referenced.

In my experience, the IRS is not in the mode of helping people out this way. It was grace that brought them that check because they needed the money to stay in school. Seminary was helping them grow, and their growth and the degrees they would receive would someday allow them to help others grow as well.

Why was the check for ten dollars more than they needed? Maybe, since our group met at a restaurant over breakfast on Thursday mornings, grace wanted to pick up the tab.

Troward's Theory Explained

Let's turn back to Thomas Troward's theory. It will help to begin by considering the difference between what we think of as "dead" matter and something we recognize as alive. A plant, such as a sunflower, has a quality that sets it apart from a piece of steel. The sunflower will turn toward the sun under its own power. When first picked, it possesses a kind of glow. This quality Troward called the life force. On the other hand, the piece of steel appears totally inert. Yet we know that at the quantum level, the steel is alive with motion. Quantum physicists tell us motion or energy is what comprises all matter. Atoms and molecules are are energy. Vibrations. Many believe the universe is alive—a living thing. When the physicist, Henry P. Stapp, was on my radio show in summer, 2008, I asked him about this. He confirmed the widely held view by quantum physicists that the universe resembles a giant thinker. I have come to picture the universe as the thought of an infinitely vast mind of organizing intelligence.

Let's get back to the sunflower. By outward appearances it is alive, and the steel is not. Few would argue this. But one might argue that a plant's state of "aliveness" is not the same as an animal's. Consider the difference in aliveness between a sunflower, an earthworm, and a goldfish. Each appears to be progressively more alive.

Now, let's add a dog, a three year old child, and a stand up comedian on the Tonight Show. Each has a progressively higher level of intelligence. So, to some extent, what we call the degree of "aliveness" can be measured by the amount of awareness or intelligence displayed—in other words, by the power of thought.

As stated before, I believe mind underlies and creates the entire universe. It's everywhere—the ground of being. But it becomes more evident to us—we can see it more clearly—as it becomes more *self-aware*. From Troward's point of view, "mind," "spirit" and "life"—or the life force—are one and the same, the distinctive quality of which is thought. He argued that the distinctive quality of matter, as in the piece of steel, is form.

Form implies the occupation of space and also limitation within certain boundaries. Thought (or life) implies neither. When we think of thought or life as existing in any particular form we associate it with the idea of occupying space, so that an elephant may be said to consist of a vastly larger amount of living substance than a mouse. But if we think of life as the fact of "aliveness," or animating spirit, we do not associate it with occupying space. The mouse is quite as much alive as the elephant, notwithstanding the difference in size. For Troward this was an important point. If we can conceive of anything as not occupying space, or as having no form, it must be present in its totality anywhere and everywhere—that is to say, at every point of space simultaneously.

The fact of thought being everywhere or non local was demonstrated by Stephan A. Schwartz, whose remote viewing seminar class, as you recall from Chapter Two, correctly identified the location and circumstances of Saddam Hussein's capture.

Schwartz conducted another experiment that demonstrates mind is everywhere at once, and that thoughts are *not* comprised of electromagnetic waves. Thoughts are in the single mind we, everything and everyone, shares. His experiment proves telepathy does not work by electromagnetic waves being sent and received like a walky-talky or radio and TV, but rather, that mind and thought are ubiquitous.

To conduct this experiment Schwartz had researchers lowered in a submarine to a water depth below which has been proven that electromagnetic waves—regardless of their frequency or strength—simply cannot penetrate. Accomplished remote viewers in the submarine got the same results about targets on the surface as did remoter viewers on the surface.

ESP / telepathy experiments were also conducted. Results between those in the sub and those on the surface were in no way diminished from what had been the case when all were located on the surface. Telepathy was thus demonstrated to be disassociated with electromagnetic waves.

In other words, ESP does not work by messages traveling from one mind to another because, as I have been saying, there is only one mind. The messages don't have to travel. All are part of it.

We and everything are aspects of this mind. What mystics have been saying for millennia is correct: *All Is One*. Being in a submarine deep below the surface of the ocean doesn't change this.

The details of this experiment can be found in Schwartz's book, *OPENING TO THE INFINITE: The Art and Science of Nonlocal Awareness* (Nemoseen Media, 2007).

The implications are difficult to wrap our thoughts around, but true. Mind does not occupy space, and it transcends time. This is how remote viewers could learn the facts of Saddam Hussein's capture months in advance, and predict the time and place Skylab would fall to earth.

The bottom line is that all mind, the life force, must exist everywhere at once in a universal here and an everlasting now.

More Evidence Mind Is Ubiquitous

The evidence clearly indicates mind—life force—is the primal stuff of the universe. This can be seen simply by observing nature. Consider a sunflower. It has no brain. According to currently accepted science, it can have no awareness. But it does have awareness. It turns its face to the sun, and it follows the sun across the sky from sunrise to dusk.

This requires some form of awareness.

Living plants are aware. Scientifically constructed, double blind experiments by researchers, including theoretical biophysicist of the University of Marburg in Germany, Fritz-Albert Popp, have demonstrated this.* And this isn't news. About 40 years ago a fellow named Cleve Backster demonstrated plants are aware by using polygraph machines. In Backster's most famous experiment, he hooked up plants in his office suite to polygraph machines, then set up a device to randomly dump a cup of living brine shrimp into a pot of boiling water. The needles on the polygraph machines would go wild each time the shrimp hit the water and went to their deaths. The plants were picking up their distress and demise.

But what led Cleve Backster to construct and carry out this experiment may be even more of an eye-opener. Lynne McTaggart, author of *The Field: The Quest for the Secret Force of the Universe,* told the following story on my show early in 2008.

Backster was and is an expert on polygraph machines and their operation—in other words, lie detectors. One evening about 40 years ago

* *Integrative Biophysics: Biophotonics* by Fritz-Albert Popp (Editor), L.V. Beloussov (Editor), Springer, February 2003

when Backster was a young man, he was sitting in his office with nothing much to do. His eyes fell on an office plant and he had an idea. He decided to hook up one of his machines to the plant and see if he could get it to react. He connected the machine and poured a glass of water into the soil around the plant. Nothing happened. The polygraph registered boredom.

Backster started thinking about what he might do to get a reaction out of the plant, and he had an idea.

"I think I'll burn one of its leaves."

At that moment, the polygraph machine went wild. The plant had reacted to his thought! The more Backster thought about burning the plant, the more the needle on the polygraph machine went ballistic.

Cleve Backster conducted many experiments along these lines which are described in his book, *Primary Perception: Bio Communication with Plants, Living Foods, and Human Cells* (White Rose Millennium Press, 2003).

People who have what's called green thumbs may think it is because they send kind thoughts to

their plants. It may be true that kind thoughts help make happy plants, but as we now know, thoughts are not sent and received. Thoughts just are—part of the mind we and everything and everyone share.

Mind Creates Matter

Troward's theory would have to be taken seriously by the scientific community if it could be demonstrated mind can produce matter.

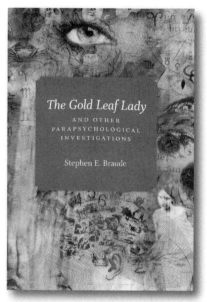

Well, you know what? It has been demonstrated. It happened in a paranormal case investigated by Stephen Braude, the University of Maryland philosophy professor whose work was discussed in Chapter Four. In one of my interviews with Professor Braude we discussed his book, *The Gold Leaf Lady and Other Parapsychological Investigations* (The University of Chicago Press, 2007).

It's about Katie, a woman born in Tennessee, the tenth of twelve children. She is apparently a simple woman. Illiterate, she lives in Florida with her husband and works as a domestic. She is also a psychic who has had documented successes helping the police solve crimes. In one instance, she was able to describe the details of the case so thoroughly and accurately, the police regarded her as a suspect until those actually responsible were apprehended.

She also apports objects—in other words, she somehow causes them to disappear in one place and reappear in another. And that's not all. Seeds reportedly germinate rapidly in her cupped hands. Observers claim to have seen her bend metal, and she is both a healer and a medium or channel. For whatever reason, her share of the life force must be of the high octane variety.

She cannot read or write in her native English, but she has been video taped writing quatrains in medieval French similar both in style and content to the actual quatrains of Nostradamus. But most amazing is what appears spontaneously on her skin—on her hands, face, arms, legs, back—apparently out of thin air. It looks like gold leaf, a thin version of the wrapping of a Hersey's Kiss.

Katie cannot control when this happens, but Dr. Braude and other witnesses have seen the foil materialize firsthand. Dr. Braude actually video taped it appearing. He has also taken the foil to be analyzed. It turns out not to be gold at all, but brass—approximately 80 percent copper and 20 percent zinc.

Katie's Subconscious Creates Brass Foil

Think about this. Her mind causes the foil to materialize. There is no other plausible explanation. In fact, Dr. Braude believes she produces brass rather than gold for a reason—albeit a subconscious one. Katie has a very difficult and tense relationship with her husband. Once she apported a carving set. It just appeared. And her husband—apparently nonplussed—said, "So what? It's not worth anything."

Soon afterward, gold colored foil began appearing on Katie's skin. But it wasn't gold, it was fool's gold—brass. Dr. Braude thinks this is how she gets back at him.

Katie doesn't know how her mind is able to make brass out of what appears to be nothing. She probably doesn't consciously know why it's brass and not some other substance. But nonetheless, her mind does it—the mind of which we all are part. Have I said it using these words, already? *Everything is created by mind. Everything is mind.*

Two Kinds of Thought, Lower and Higher

How does this help us understand how there can be life between lives, and how those children got the birthmarks?

First, Troward would point out that there are two kinds of thought. We might call them lower and higher, or subjective and objective because what differentiates the higher from the lower is the recognition of self. A plant, a worm, and perhaps a goldfish possess the lower kind only. They are unaware of self. Perhaps a dog, and certainly a boy and a comedian possess both. The higher variety of self-aware thought is possessed in progressively larger amounts as if ascending a scale.

Troward believed the lower mode of thought, the subjective, is the subconscious intelligence—or mind—present everywhere that, among other things, supports and controls the mechanics of life in every species and in every individual. It causes plants to grow toward the sun and to push roots into the soil. It causes hearts to beat and lungs to take in air without our having to think about it. This ubiquitous subjective mind controls all of the so-called involuntary functions of the body.

That this lower kind of thought is everywhere at once coincides with Carl Jung's theory that we humans share a Universal Mind. Moreover, we each have our own portion, our individual subconscious mind that blends into the collective mind. We also have a conscious mind, the producer of objective thought that makes us self-aware. The two types of mind are inextricably linked in that our conscious mind arises out of the subconscious and remains linked to it. The gradual emergence of self-aware thought out of the universal subconscious mind over the course of evolution is implicit in our consideration of the plant, earthworm, goldfish, dog, boy, comedian and so forth up the scale.

Our conscious minds are an aspect of our individual morphogenetic field hypothesized by Rupert Sheldrake, and our individual field is part of the larger field of our particular birth family. Genes determine our hair and skin color and the color of our eyes, but or family's morphogenetic field determines the form our bodies take, such as the shapes of our noses and our ears. The field of our family is in turn part of the morphogenetic field of humankind, and so on up the ladder to include all living things, Gaia—the earth, and ultimately, the universe.

Who are we? In each life we are a combination of the conscious mind or soul that carries over from previous lives, the genes and morphogenetic field of the family we are born into, and the environment into which we were born and raised. More fundamentally, we are sparks of the Universal Mind experiencing itself.

How the Reincarnates Got Their Birthmarks

How can we be born missing a limb we lost in the previous life or with birthmarks that mimic the wound we died from? As Troward believed, our conscious or objective mind must have power over the subjective mind. This can be seen in the phenomenon of hypnosis, which works because the hypnotist bypasses his subject's conscious mind and speaks directly to his subject's subconscious (subjective) mind. The subconscious has no choice but to bring into reality that which is communicated directly to it as fact by a conscious mind.

Being totally subjective, the subconscious mind cannot step outside of itself for an objective look. The result is that the subconscious (subjective) mind is entirely under the control of the conscious (objective) mind. As a result, the subconscious will work diligently to support or to bring into reality whatever the conscious mind believes to be true. A person's subjective mind must be at work as his fetus grows. The result is that if we believe we have missing fingers, a leg or a hand, we will be missing a leg, a hand or fingers, when we are born.

The implications of this are staggering. As many have been saying for quite some time, our beliefs literally create our personal realities.

Here's some advice. Next time you are between lives, if you have lost some body part in the life just past, think yourself a new one before you reincarnate. Or take the time to process the life just past, and resist the temptation to return to the physical realm too quickly.

Get Ready for Pseudo Skeptics to Throw up a lot of Flack

While I believe Julie Beischel's work combines with that of Ian Stevenson, Jim Tucker and others reported upon in this book to form an an airtight case for the continuation of consciousness, I am equally certain the pseudo skeptics will continue to hold onto and profess the view that death is the end. I expect they will do so even though there are no dangling straws for them to grasp.

I believe this to be the case for two reasons. The first has to do with self preservation. Some of these skeptics have, perhaps unwittingly, been teaching classes and writing books full of erroneous information for years. Throwing the old paradigm on the trash heap of history may likewise place them and their reputations on the trash heap.

The second is that some may have good reason to want to believe consciousness does not continue. These folks may be afraid they will be judged after death. Because of this, they may prefer to remain in a state of denial.

They should not, however, fear the judgment of others. Near death experiencers report the only judging done during the life review is by the individual undergoing the review. Others present at the review may offer advice or solace, but they heed Jesus' command: "Do not judge or you too will be judged." (Matthew 7:1)

Of course, it's true we can be harsher judges of ourselves than impartial observers might be. I for one am guilty of things in my youth I'm not looking forward to reviewing.

But, when all is said and done, think of the good the realization consciousness lives on will do. At last we will come to the realization we are eternal. Think how that will change someone who now thinks otherwise. It's got to make him or her see the world differently.

How Will Knowing You Are Eternal Change You?

How about you? What will you do differently now that you know?

No longer will it be necessary to fear death—unless you are worried about your judgment of yourself. But now that you know, you can do something about it. Find the people you harmed and make amends. And change your life: "Give to the poor and you will have treasure in heaven." (Matthew 19:21)

You no longer have to feel the great sense of loss you may have felt in the past when someone you love dies. You will see them again.

You can chuck the mid-life crises, knowing you will have the opportunity for another go at youth in a future life.

We can all come to view death for what many have long believed it to be: a transition, rather than the end.

No longer will it be viewed as a particularly good idea to keep someone alive artificially on life support, who has no chance to recover, and is suffering.

And consider this. Pregnant women are taught how to give birth. It will likewise make sense for everyone to learn how to die as comfortably as possible. It will also make sense to teach people what to expect when they do.

Look for the light. Go to it.

Facts that Demonstrate Consciousness Continues after Death

1. Persons who experience clinical death during surgical operations and are revived frequently report leaving their bodies and observing them being worked on. Often they relate conversations by doctors and details about the operating room and equipment being used that could not have been obtained via the ordinary bodily senses of sight and hearing.

2. The memories of past lives of more than 2500 children have been researched by the University of Virginia and found to match the lives of the people the children claimed to have been, all of whom died prior to the childrens' births.

3. Missing or mutilated body parts of the person in the previous life often correspond to birth defects present in the child remembering the past life.

4. Birthmarks corresponding to fatal wounds, such as entrance and exit gunshot wounds, have been observed in more than 200 cases.

5. Children recalling past lives frequently show personal traits as well as food and other preferences that are at odds with their current family and environment. These can often be attributed to the prior personality.

5. Children recalling past lives frequently possess phobias that relate to the cause of death in the previous life such as a fear of water in the case of drowning or a fear of firearms if the death was from a gunshot wound.

6. Reincarnation is the only possible explanation that fits all the data and circumstances in the more than 2500 cases researched and solved by the University of Virginia.

7. In strictly controlled quintuple blind tests by the Windbridge Institute, in which the possibility of fraud is eliminated, mediums are able to report accurate information about people who are no longer living.

8. Psychic mediums report that the qualitative experience of interaction with discarnates is different than that of reporting on living persons. Often they sense a presence, suggesting communication directly with the discarnate rather than the use of clairvoyance or other psychic phenomena.

The Argument Against the Continuance of Consciousness

It does not square with the nineteenth and twentieth century materialist-reductionist tenet that consciousness is a product of the brain.

What a man believes upon grossly insufficient evidence is an index into his desires—desires of which he himself is often unconscious. If a man is offered a fact which goes against his instincts, he will scrutinize it closely, and unless the evidence is overwhelming, he will refuse to believe it. If, on the other hand, he is offered something which affords a reason for acting in accordance to his instincts, he will accept it even on the slightest evidence.

Bertrand Russell
(1872-1970)

Chapter Ten
Why Accepting the Truth Can
Be Difficult

Why is it so difficult for some of us to believe in life after death? We have discussed why some skeptics may never give up their position, but what about those who would like to believe but cannot bring themselves to do so?

I'd say a main reason is that it's hard to shake off what one has been taught since kindergarten. The science of life we learned in school is based on an erroneous tenet—that consciousness and intelligence came about as results of evolution. The truth is the other way around. Evolution came about as a result of consciousness and intelligence.

A quick summary of what we were taught goes like this: First RNA, then DNA came along. This happened by accident. One celled animals formed in the sea and became more complex over time as traits developed that helped them survive. Random mutations produced ever more complex organisms that won the battles for survival. The fittest were able to propagate and pass on their genes. Eventually, some crawled out of the sea and evolution continued on land. Brains—which had happened by accident and gave their owners big advantages over the brainless—became more complex and created awareness and intelligence.

In a nutshell, that's what we learned. But it seems more logical, given what we now know, that consciousness and intelligence came first and are the bedrock of all that is. Evolution was helped along by grace, which is a phenomenon of the life force, or ground of being.

Let me tell you what makes sense to me based on everything we know that's been set down in this book up to now.

In the beginning only one consciousness existed—only one mind. Now, many separate consciousnesses exist. Sentient beings have their own unique consciousness as a result of evolution.

Consciousness is not caused by electrons jumping across synapses. Consciousness just is. Some of it became separated into unique souls as morphogenetic fields formed in the primal consciousness, or ground of being. This ground of being is the clay evolution molded into who we are—a result of the long journey up from RNA, DNA, and the first sparks of consciousness that formed one celled creatures in the sea.

Mystics refer to sparks being cast out from the Tao or godhead. They are referring to the differentiated consciousness of these morphogenetic fields. Primitive morphogenetic fields became more and more complex over time as they adapted to their environments in their quest for growth and survival. As the millennia passed, portions of the ground of being of consciousness evolved objective awareness.

Parenthetically, this may be how the universe reproduces itself—sort of like an amoeba dividing and subdividing and dividing again. Even though we are separate, however, we nonetheless remain connected to and part of the ground of being from which we came—just as a TV channel remains part of the complete ban of TV channel frequencies.

Our bodily senses make us feel separate. These are necessary, of course, for us to function in the physical realm. We need them to operate our bodies. In the East the sense of separation is seen as an illusion created by the senses called "Maya."

Created in the Likeness of Our Creator

Consciousness, the ground of being, is the bedrock of all that is. But for it to enter into and experience physical reality requires a brain and a body. Once encapsulated in a body, consciousness experiences primarily through the focal point of the brain via the medium of eyes, ears, sense of smell, taste and touch. It seems this nexus is where consciousness is located. In a way it is, but remote viewing and retrieval of information through psychic means are still possible because we remain at all times part of the one mind. Sentient beings are focal points of consciousness within the the larger consciousness, and some can access information from the larger, ocean of consciousness. This is because all is connected. All is one.

Mystics have been saying "All Is One" for millennia. On my radio show, I have had a number of people describe the experience of spontaneously realizing this. For some it was brought about when they were out in nature and experienced a sunrise or a sunset. For others it happened at the birth of a child, or as a result of a near death experience.

In his book, *The Rebirth of Nature, The Greening of Science and God,* Rupert Sheldrake quotes a woman, an art teacher, who recounted an experience she had while walking on the Pangbourne Moors at the age of five. I quoted this in my book *THE TRUTH,* and will do so again here. She puts into words what I believe many of us have felt at one time or another but perhaps later dismissed when our "rational" minds again got the upper hand:

Suddenly I seemed to see the mist as a shimmering gossamer tissue and the harebells, appearing here and there, seemed to shine with a brilliant fire. Somehow I understood that this was the living tissue of life itself, in which all that we call consciousness is embedded, appearing here and there as a shining focus of energy in the more diffused whole. In that moment I knew that I had my special place, as had all other things, animate and so-called inanimate, and that we were all part of this universal tissue which was both fragile yet immensely strong, and utterly good and beneficent.

Until now, people came to the realization of oneness and that life is eternal through an epiphany, as happened above. Now there are facts—the facts set down in this book—that make it possible to come to the realization through logic. How quickly an individual comes to this will depend, I believe, on his or her personality type. I will attempt to explain.

The Myers-Briggs personality approach has four dimensions:

I or E (Introspective versus Extroverted)

N or S (Intuition versus Sensation as a preference for information gathering and decision making, i.e., Intuitive versus Sensible—sensible in the strict meaning of the word as in perceiving through the senses.)

T or F (Thinking or Feeling)

J or P (Judging or Perceiving)

My personality type is INTJ. So I'm introspective, prefer intuition, like to use rational thought rather than feelings when considering things, and I'm constantly judging stuff rather than passively perceiving it. One way this manifests is that what makes sense to me is much more important that who said it. Some people don't like having me around because of this—my cross to bear. They have the feeling I see through them, like the little boy who shouted, "The king has no clothes!" while everyone else was thinking, "The king *must* have clothes. After all, he's the *king*. It *must* be *me* who just can't see them."

Less than two percent of the population is like me. Every personality type has its good points and unique abilities. We INTJs are known as builders of theoretical models. We see life as a giant chess game—understanding it and winning simply require arranging the pieces properly.

Of the four dimensions, the N versus S is the largest source of misunderstandings and hard feelings. The intuitive person often finds complex ideas coming to him as a complete whole. It is then up to him or her to reverse engineer these ideas in order to determine why they are true. Sensibles go at things from the other direction, which means they are likely to want more data than an intuitive will think necessary.

Ian Stevenson may have been a Sensible. He collected and verified more than 2500 reports of children's reports of past lives. An Intuitive, having soon recognized a pattern, would have stopped after investigating and verifying a dozen or so. The main reason to collect more would be to convince the Sensibles. Of course, this may be why Stevenson did so.

Only 25 percent of the population is Intuitive. The big majority, 75 percent, are Sensibles. It seems to me 2500 confirmed cases ought to be enough to convince even the most ardent Sensible.

How about you? Are you convinced? If not, there may be another reason. Let's look into that one.

People Are Hardwired to Not Change Their Minds

Sensibles aren't the only ones who don't change their minds easily when presented with new information. People are not easily swayed who already have a hard and fast opinion about the way things. This has been demonstrated through scientific research.

Drew Westen, Ph.D.

For years, Drew Westen, a psychologist at Emory University, has been studying how people think, particularly in the area of politics. For my money, those who hold steadfastly to the old ideas of materialism in the face of data indicating a universe comprised of something we can't see are much like members of a political party who refuse to see where their own party or candidate has veered off track.

In experiments using MRI scans, Westen has demonstrated that persons with partisan preferences believe what they want to believe regardless of the facts. Not only that, they unconsciously congratulate themselves—the reward centers of their brains light up—when they reject new information that does not square with their predetermined views.

In one test, subjects were presented with contradictory statements made by George Bush and John Kerry. Republicans judged Kerry's flip-flop harshly, while letting Bush off the hook for his. Democrats did the reverse. Interestingly, brain scans showed that the parts of the brain accounting for emotion were far more active during the experiment than the reasoning parts.

Anyone who follows politics will not be surprised by this. The truth is, Westen's research does not relate anything new. Solzhenitsyn characterized this phenomenon as "the desire not to know." In 1915 George Santayana acknowledged in a letter to his sister that "when I read [newspapers] I form perhaps a new opinion of the newspaper but seldom a new opinion on the subject discussed." Westen's research has value because it backs up impressions with empirical facts—brain scans.

In another experiment Westen conducted before the 2004 presidential election, participants were told a soldier at Abu Ghraib was charged with torturing prisoners and wanted to subpoena Bush administration officials. Different participants were given different amounts of evidence supporting the soldier's claim that he had been told the administration had suspended Geneva Convention rules regarding treatment of prisoners. But it didn't matter how much information they had.

Westen said, "Eight-four percent of the time, we could predict whether people believed the evidence was sufficient to subpoena Donald Rumsfeld based on just three things: the extent to which they liked Republicans, the extent to which they liked human rights groups like Amnesty International, and the extent to which they liked the U.S. military."

Results such as this might help explain why some debates never seem to end. People are invested in the positions they take. So, as Westen puts it, they have a tendency to weigh not just the facts, but also, "what they would feel if they came to one conclusion or another, and they often come to the conclusion that would make them feel better, no matter what the facts are."

Now that you know this, I hope you will set anything you learned in school or elsewhere aside, and truly consider what's presented in this book.

Here [in this experience] all blades of grass, wood, and stone, all
things are One . . . when is a man in mere understanding?
When he sees one thing separated from another.
And when is he above mere understanding?
When he sees all in all, then a man stands
above mere understanding.

Meister Eckhart
(c. 1260–c. 1328)

Chapter Eleven
High Time for a Paradigm Shift

One reason it's hard to accept that consciousness continues after death is that it requires scrapping the materialistic model of the world most of us still hold. But it's important to understand models are just that—approximations of how things are. This chapter will explain how the current model developed. The chapter that follows will offer a new one into which the continuation of consciousness fits comfortably.

Whether we realize it or not, we each have a world view—or a model of how things work. You might think of this as a stack of cans that forms a pyramid you might see as a grocery store aisle end display. Each can represents an individual belief. Each belief in the display supports other beliefs. Try to change a foundational belief, and the whole thing may come tumbling down. That's why I will offer you an entirely new model of the world so you can replace the whole thing at once.

As we will soon see, in the past century scientists have been presented with information that would require tearing down and rebuilding from the ground up the model they hold of reality. Rather than do so, most have taken the easy way by dismissing as anomalies information that does not fit. We saw in the last chapter that this reaction is common. If enough of these so-called anomalies build up, however, they can be like water backing up behind a dam. Eventually, that dam has to burst. I believe that time has come.

Let's start by taking a look at how we got to the world view, or model, that's about to be washed downstream.

A Very Old World View

There was a time, anthropologists tell us, when humans felt at one with nature. This can still be seen today in primitive cultures. Called pantheism, humans felt they were an integral part of the ecosystem. The Divine showed itself in many forms and was present in all things.

But as humans grew more self aware, they began to feel separation. The myth of Adam and Eve recalls the time when humans parted company with the view that they could commune with the Divine. They cut the cord by exercising free will.

No longer seeing God in themselves and in others, we humans conjured up gods outside ourselves. In ancient Greece, for example, many gods representing various human qualities were thought to exist. The world view that evolved in those ancient times had man in the middle between two worlds—a place the Chinese referred to as the Middle Kingdom. The gods lived above the clouds of Mt. Olympus, although they did come to earth now and then, mostly to cause problems for humans.

Below the Middle Kingdom—what caused it to be in the middle—was the underworld, home of the dead, where Hades was in charge and the three headed dog Cereberus guarded a gate one got to after crossing the River Styx.

Different cultures had different takes on this three layered universe. Then as now, ideas about God and gods differed depending on the group one belonged to. The Egyptians had Bal. The Jews had the god of Abraham. The Romans and the Greeks had a pantheon full.

The Idea of One God Evolved and with It a New World View

Then came Jesus of Nazareth and the idea emerged that only one God ruled over creation—although He did have angels and eventually saints who took up some of the positions left vacant by departing Roman and Greek gods.

In 1994 Karen Armstrong published a book, *A History of God,* that chronicled history of the emergence of the concept of one God.

Karen Armstrong

Because of this idea, the world view changed somewhat. God and angels replaced the pantheon of gods above the clouds. A fallen angel, Satan, replaced Hades. The place below the ground became hell rather than the underworld—where evildoers went. The good folk would be raised at the end of time on judgment day and given new, light bodies.

This view held sway for better than a thousand years but was destined to change again because of a new scientific discovery by Christopher Columbus (1451-1506).

Columbus lived on high ground overlooking a Mediterranean harbor. I have visited the ruin of what is said to be the house where he grew up. In that part of the world there is almost no humidity and the air is very clear. If Columbus had good eyes, he would not even have needed a spyglass to see ships climb up over the horizon as they approached the harbor. I've witnessed this myself. Columbus could see the world was round and he must have decided to prove it by sailing west to get to the spice islands of the East Indies.

Columbus never realized it himself, but he didn't actually get there. Nevertheless, some of Ferdinand Magellan's (1480-1521) crew did, and beyond. Of the 237 men who set out on five ships in 1519, 18 actually completed the circumnavigation of the globe and returned to Spain in 1522.

Christopher Columbus (1451-1506)

The newly realized fact that the world was round forced the then commonly held world view to change. Nevertheless, since people and, most important, Church leaders believed that God had created it, the earth remained at the center of the universe. Now heaven, the dwelling place of God, was seen as being somewhere above the stars. Hell was still beneath the ground, down where it was hot, the place from which molten lava spewed when volcanos erupted.

The World View Gets an Update

Nicolaus Copernicus (1473-1543)

It wasn't long before this world view had to be updated. A fellow named Nicolaus Copernicus (1473-1543) determined the sun was at the center of the solar system. But the Church—the authority back then as science is today—pretty much ignored this concept because it did not go along with accepted canon. This "look the other way" tactic will be seen time and again in the twentieth century.

Then, a century later, along came Galileo Galilei (1564–1642), a man who would not leave well enough alone. Galileo—among other things an astronomer—championed Copernicus's assertion as proven fact. As a result, Galileo started having to watch his back. This was heresy. At that time people were being burned at the stake for less. Indeed, the leaders of the

**Galileo Galilei
(1564-1642)**

Church told Galileo he'd better recant, and he did. As a result, Galileo got off easy, spending the final years of his life under house arrest on orders of the Inquisition.

But even the Church couldn't keep word from getting out. Gradually, the accepted views of the day began to change.

A Tiny World Comes into View

In 1675, a Dutchman named Antoni van Leeuwenhoek (1632-1723) — an amateur lens grinder and microscope builder—saw for the first time tiny organisms he called "animalcules" living in stagnant water. He also spotted them in scum collected from his teeth. Leeuwenhock didn't know or even speculate that "animalcules" might cause disease. It took until the nineteenth century for that revelation to dawn. At the time, the idea creatures so small they were invisible to the naked eye entered the body to make a person sick and sometimes die would have seemed totally absurd. It was thought demons and the devil caused such things, or that God did it to punish sinners. In 1692 in Salem, MA, 18 were hanged and one was crushed to death because they were thought to be witches in league with Satan. No wonder after that, and down until today, the idea of Satan and demons and witchcraft was thought to be pure supersti-

Antoni van Leeuwenhoek (1632-1723)

tion. To believe in such things was to invite witch hunts and mass hysteria, and nobody wanted that.

The Age of Reason Dawns

Thomas Hobbes (1588-1679)

Even so, a new day was dawning, a period alternately referred to as "The Age of Enlightenment" and "The Age of Reason." English philosopher, Thomas Hobbes (1588-1679), had argued that aside from God—the "first cause" who created the material world—nothing existed that is not of the material world. The logic he used was simple. How could it if God created everything?

This view was ultimately to lead to the great clock maker theory, the idea that God created the universe, wound it up, let it go, and was no longer involved in its operation. Natural laws also had been created that kept going what had been set in motion. Called Deism, many founding fathers, including my personal hero, Thomas Jefferson, subscribed to this view. Jefferson, by the way, was an INTJ.

Hobbes had a big impact on the Age of Enlightenment, which was to pick up steam in the eighteenth century. But the big kahuna was Sir Isaac Newton (1643 – 1727), an English physicist, mathematician, astronomer, natural philosopher, alchemist, and theologian. Certainly one of the most influential men of all time, his *Philosophiæ Naturalis Principia Mathematica,*

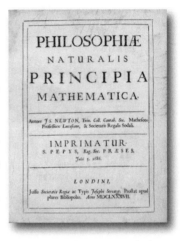

published in 1687, is considered to be the groundwork for most of classical mechanics. Newton described universal gravitation and the three laws of motion which dominated the scientific view of the physical universe at least until the advent of quantum mechanics. It seems safe to say Thomas Hobbes's materialistic view of reality coupled with Newton's mechanistic view is the bedrock of scientific thinking today, except among quantum physicists.

Sir Isaac Newton
(1643-1727)

The prevailing world view that emerged from the Age of Reason was that the universe might be compared to a giant machine. The Sun was at the center of the solar system. The Earth and planets revolved around it. Nothing existed but the material world. What was thought of in the seventeenth century and before as the invisible world of spirit did not exist. Everything that happened had a logical cause. Natural laws governed everything.

Darwin's Theory Takes Hold

In 1859 an Englishman, Charles Darwin, published *On the Origin of Species,* a seminal work in scientific literature and a landmark work in evolutionary biology. Its full title, *On the Origin of Species by Means of Natural Selection, or the Preservation of Favoured Races in the Struggle for Life,* uses the term "races" to mean biological varieties. Darwin's book introduced the theory that populations evolve over the course of generations through a process of

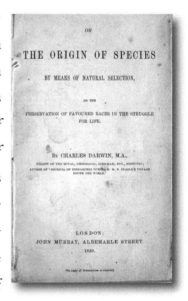

natural selection. It presented a body of evidence indicating the diversity of life arose through a branching pattern of evolution and common descent. In other words, God had not created the variety of life on the planet, nor had He created humans. All this had happened through a natural—what might be seen as mechanical—process. This became accepted as fact among the educated classes.

But astute scientists then and now realized something important was missing from Darwin's theory. It cannot be reconciled with the second law of thermodynamics, or Law of Entropy—the fact that in a closed system things tend to break down and fall apart, rather than get better. In other words, your old car is not going to get better by itself. It's going to require outside help, meaning you are going to have to write a check or pull out a credit card.

Charles Darwin
(1809–1882)

How then could life get more complex by accident? What caused an eye, a kidney, a heart, ears, and all those complex systems to develop? We can guess from the theories outlined in this book it has something to do with the life force—the underlying intelligence, subjective mind, push-me pull-me effect coupled with grace. That's now. But only Thomas Troward considered such things back then. Most ignored his theory and overlooked the flaw. Many still do today.

Darwin's theories reinforced the rationalist idea that the so called supernatural was a figment of human imagination and—not wanting to be burned at the stake—most scientists probably wanted to keep it safely buried. Life and its diversity were results of a natural process known as survival of the fittest coupled with the environment in which a particular species had evolved. Intelligence and mind had evolved as life had evolved and had reached its pinnacle in humans. Mind and intelligence were produced by an organ, the brain, which had resulted from this evolution. Thought was created by the brain and would later be envisioned as being a result of electrons jumping across synapses. It was contained within the skull. ESP was impossible and so was magic.

A Wedge Between Science and Religion Is Hammered in

With this world view, a wedge was inserted and hammered in between science, religion and any possibility of things so called supernatural. Hobbes had said nothing existed but the physical. If this were so, where could God possibly reside? What about the heavenly hosts? Thought was contained within the skull so what possible good could prayer do?

A line was drawn. Educated men and women could not believe in God and prayer or angels or ghosts and demons, which were seen as figments of ignorance and superstition. Many may have had a yearning for God—as humans seem to for the spiritual—but could not rationalize His existence. All were forced to choose between religion and science, though many attempted to straddle the line—as they still do today.

Now, in the early part of the twenty-first century, this world view continues to be the only socially acceptable one in some circles. But there are signs it is beginning to crumble. Hundreds of thousands, perhaps millions, have shifted to a new world view based on a new branch of science called quantum mechanics and the findings of scientific research that do not fit the materialist-reductionist mold. I hope this book will do its part to knock that view down once and for all.

Let's look at some of the pioneers who have not been afraid to speak out, as well as their ideas and discoveries that conflict with the prevailing nineteenth-twentieth century world view. The following does not in any way represent an exhaustive list. My apologies to anyone who feels left out, and to anyone who thinks I have overlooked a key figure.

Matter = Energy

**Albert Einstein
(1879-1955)**

In 1905 Albert Einstein (1879-1955), a German-born theoretical physicist, published a paper proving that light behaves both as a wave and as particles. This, as well as Einstein's famous formula, $E = MC^2$, indicates reality and matter are not what they seem. Matter or mass as it is referred to in this formula is equivalent to energy and vice versa.

In 1912 Swiss psychiatrist Carl Jung (1875-1961) published *Wandlungen und Symbole der Libido* (known in English as *The Psychology of the Unconscious)* that postulated a collective unconscious, sometimes known as collective subconscious. According to Jung there is an unconscious

**Carl Jung
(1875-1961)**

mind shared by a society, a people, or all humanity, that is the product of ancestral experience and contains such concepts as the classic archetypes, science, religion, and morality.

Quantum physicists came along who expanded on Eintstein's work. Niels Henrik David Bohr, a Danish physicist, made fundamental contributions to understanding atomic structure and quantum mechanics, for which he received the Nobel Prize in Physics in 1922. He is quoted as having said, "Everything we call real is made of things that cannot be regarded as real."

Nothing is really solid. Everything is energy—vibrations.

**Niels Bohr
(1885 – 1962)**

ESP and Psychokinesis Are Proven Real

**J. B Rhine
(1895 – 1980)**

As we know from our earlier discussion, in the early 1930s a man named J. B. (Joseph Banks) Rhine moved from Harvard University to Duke to set up a parapsychology laboratory. Rhine not only founded the parapsychology lab at Duke, he also founded the *Journal of Parapsychology* and the Foundation for Research on the Nature of Man. His double blind studies conducted largely between 1930 and 1960 established that ESP exists and is real. Not mentioned in our earlier discussion, they also showed psychokinesis—mind over matter—is real as well, at least to a small degree.

His findings were either scoffed at or ignored by the scientific community then as they continue to be today.

Zen Is Introduced to the West

In 1953, Eugen Herrigel (1884-1955), a German philosopher who taught philosophy at Tohoku Imperial University in Sendai, Japan, from 1924-1929 published the book, *Zen and the Art of Archery*. This introduced Zen Buddhism to the West and the concept that "All Is One," i.e., everything is connected rather than made up of separate parts. How else could Zen masters shoot arrows while blindfolded and consistently hit the bull's-eyes of targets many yards away?

In 1966 a British philosopher named Alan Watts (1915-1973) published a book called *The Book: On the Taboo Against Knowing Who You Are* that went into detail about Buddhist thought. Known as an interpreter and popularizer of Asian philosophies for a Western audience, Watts wrote more than 25 books and numerous articles on subjects such as personal identity, the true nature of reality,

**Alan Watts
(1915 – 1975)**

higher consciousness and the meaning of life. His writings and ideas fueled a new movement which came to be known as New Age.

Plants Tune into Thoughts

As discussed, a polygraph expert named Cleve Backster (born 1924) began research in 1966 that demonstrated living plants tune into the thoughts and intentions of humans as well as other aspects of their environments, thus indicating some sort of hidden mental connection between living things. His findings were ridiculed, but have since been confirmed by other researchers.

In 1978 a young man with a B.A., M.A., and Ph.D. from the University of Virginia and an M.D. from Georgia Medical School named Raymond Moody (born 1944) published a book called *Life After Life,* in which he detailed the experiences of people who had been clinically dead and resuscitated.

The Phenomenon of Grace Is Publicized

Also in 1978, a psychiatrist named M. Scott Peck (1936-2005) published a book that became a huge bestseller called, *The Road Less Travelled: A New Psychology Of Love, Traditional Values And Spiritual Growth.* Among other things, Peck's book dealt with the phenomenon of grace, which we covered in the last chapter. He said grace was both common and to a certain extent, predictable. He also wrote that,

**M. Scott Peck
(1936 – 2005)**

"grace will remain unexplainable within the conceptual framework of conventional science and 'natural law' as we understand it."

Grace is the unseen force that brings the best possible results out of unfortunate events and circumstances, .i.e., "every cloud has a silver lining." In Peck's own words, "There is a force, the mechanism of which we do not fully understand, that seems to operate routinely in most people to protect and encourage their physical health even under the most adverse conditions." His book gives specific examples.

It seems to me, grace is the life force at work.

Quantum Physics Is Introduced to the Masses

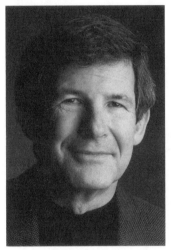

Gary Zukav

In 1979, Gary Zukav, a former Green Beret during the war in Vietnam, published a book called the *Dancing Wu Li Masters: An Overview of the New Physics.* Targeted for laymen, it explained the basics of quantum physics in everyday language, i.e., without the use of complicated mathematics. Zukav concluded that "the philosophical implication of quantum mechanics is that all of the things in our universe (including us) that appear to exist independently are actually parts of one all-encompassing organic pattern, and that no parts of that pattern are ever really separate from it or from each other."

Also in 1979, James Lovelock published a book called *Gaia: A New Look at Life on Earth* that explained his idea that life on earth functions as a single organism. In contrast to the conventional belief that living matter is passive in the face of threats to its existence, the book explored the hypothesis that the earth's living matter—air, ocean, and land surfaces—forms a complex system that has the capacity to keep the

Earth a fit place for life. Since Gaia was first published, many of Jim Lovelock's predictions have come true.

The Spiritual Dimension Is Explored

In the mid 1980s a television series appeared on PBS called *The Power of Myth*, featuring author and Sarah Lawrence College Comparative Religion Professor, Joseph Campbell (1904-1987). These programs made an impact on a significant segment of the public and opened their eyes to the possibility of the existence of what might be termed "a spiritual dimension." This can be summed up using Campbell's own words, "Anyone who has had an experience of mystery knows there is a dimension of the universe that is not available to his senses."

**Joseph Campbell
(1904-1987)**

Scientific Studies Demonstrate the Efficacy of Prayer

In July, 1988, Dr. Randolph Byrd, a cardiologist, published an article in the *Southern Medical Journal* about the effects of prayer on cardiac patients. Over a ten-month period, he used a computer to assign 393 patients admitted to the coronary care unit at San Francisco General Hospital either to a group that was prayed for by home prayer groups (192 patients), or to a group that was not prayed for (201). A double blind test, neither the patients, doctors, nor the nurses knew which group a patient was in.

The patients who were remembered in prayer had remarkably, and a statistically significant number of better experiences and outcomes than those who were not prayed for. Also, fewer prayed-for patients died, although the difference between groups in this case was not large enough to be considered statistically significant.

In 1994 Rupert Sheldrake, a British biochemist whose theory has already been discussed, published a book called *A New Science of Life.* The editors of the British journal, *Nature,* called this book, "the best candidate for burning there has been for many years."

What Researchers Know Can Determine the Outcome

In 1995, Raymond Chiao, a Hong Cong native and quantum physicist then teaching at the University of California at Berkeley, published a paper about a series of experiments. The paper, reported upon in the July 19 issue of *Newsweek* magazine, said that what researchers knew or

Richard Feynman, Ph.D.

did not know about certain aspects of each experiment had a predictable determination on their outcomes. In other words, what was in the researchers' minds—i.e. thought—apparently determined the result. In the *Newsweek* article reporting on this, Nobel Prize winning physicist Richard Feynman was quoted as having said this is the "central mystery" of quantum mechanics, that something as intangible as knowledge—in this case, which slit a photon went through—changes something as concrete as a pattern on a screen.

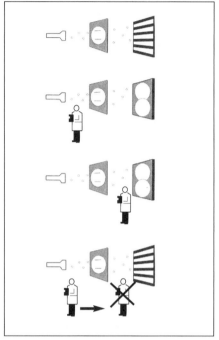

In 2001, F. Holmes Atwater published the book already discussed detailing how in 1979 he set up and managed—until his retirement from the Army in 1988—a remote viewing unit of U. S. Army intelligence.

What the researcher knows or doesn't know determines the pattern on the screen.

Prayer Adds Fuel to the Life Force

Also in 2001, a study published in the September issue of the *Journal of Reproductive Medicine* showed that prayer was able to double the success rate of in vitro fertilization procedures that lead to pregnancy. The findings revealed that a group of women who had people praying for them had a 50 percent pregnancy rate compared to a 26 percent rate in the group of women who did not have anyone praying for them. In the study—led by Rogerio Lobo, chairman of obstetrics and gynecology at Columbia University's College of Physi-

Columbia University Library

cians & Surgeons—none of the women undergoing the IVF procedures knew about the prayers on their behalf. Nor did their doctors. In fact, the 199 women were in Cha General Hospital in Seoul, Korea, thousands of miles from those praying for them in the U.S., Canada and Australia. This collaborates with other studies and quantum physics theory that distance is not a factor at the subatomic level of mind.

Research Tells How Best to Pray

An organization exists that has as its purpose the study of what prayer techniques produce the best results. It's called Spindrift* and was founded by Christian Science practitioners who have been at this since 1975.

The first question Spindrift researchers sought to answer is, does prayer work? The answer, as we already know, is yes. In one test, rye seeds were split into groupings of equal numbers and placed in a shallow container on a soil-like substance called vermiculite. (For city dwellers, this is commonly used by gardeners.) A string was drawn across the middle to indicate that the seeds were divided into side A and side B. Side A was prayed for. Side B was not. A statistically greater number of rye shoots emerged from side A than from side B.

Variations of this experiment were devised and conducted, but not until this one was repeated by many different Christian Science prayer practitioners all of whom got consistent results.

Next, salt was added to the water supply. Different batches of rye seeds received doses of salt ranging from one teaspoon per eight cups

---

* See http://www.spindriftresearch.org.

of water to four teaspoons per eight cups. Doses were stepped up in increments of one-half teaspoon per batch.

A total of 2.3 percent more seeds sprouted on the prayed-for side of the first batch—one teaspoon per half-gallon of water—than on the unprayed-for side—800 "prayed-for" seeds sprouted out of 2,000, versus 778 sprouts out of 2000 in the not-prayed-for side. As the dosage of salt was increased, the total number of seeds sprouting decreased, but the proportion of seeds that sprouted on the prayed-for sides increased, compared to the unprayed-for sides, as the amount of the salt—stress—increased. In the 1.5 teaspoon batch, the increase was 3.3 percent. In the 2.0 teaspoon batch, 13.8 percent. In the 2.5 batch, 16.5 percent. In the 3.0, 30.8 percent. Five times as many prayed-for seeds in the 3.5 batch sprouted—although the total number which sprouted was small as can be seen from the chart below. Finally, no seeds sprouted in the 4.0 teaspoon per eight cup batch.

What this says is what people lying in a ditch with bombs going off around them have always known: the more dire the situation, the more helpful prayer will be. Up to a point. There comes a time when things are so bad nothing helps.

Salt	Control/Grown		Prayed-for / Grown		% Increase
1.0	2,000	778	2,000	800	2.3
1.5	3,000	302	3,000	312	3.3
2.0	3,000	217	3,000	247	13.8
2.5	3,000	454	3,000	528	16.3
3.0	3,000	52	3,000	68	30.8
3.5	2,000	2	2,000	10	400.0
4.0	3,000	0	3,000	0	0.0

Studies similar to this have been and are being carried out by a consortium of scientists put together by Lynne McTaggart, author of the book published in 2002, *THE FIELD: The Quest for the Secret Force of the Universe,* and her 2008 release, *The INTENTION EXPERIMENT: Using Your Thoughts to Change Your Life and the World.* When she was on my show in early 2008, she described some of these experiments and the terrific success she

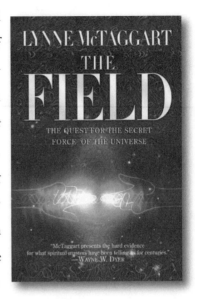

and her colleagues have had. She said several of these studies were already being prepared for publication.

Mind Is Shown to Create Matter

In 2007, Stephen E. Braude published the book already discussed, *The Gold Leaf Lady and Other Parapsychological Investigations.* The book tells the story of Katie, a woman who demonstrates mind can produce matter—in this case brass: 80% copper and 20% zinc with its huge implications for quantum physics and he origins of the physical universe.

Mediums Can Relate Accurate Information about the Dead

Also in 2008, Julie Beischel, Ph.D., whose work was covered in Chapter Three, published a paper in *The Journal of Parapsychology* in which she concluded, " . . . certain mediums can report accurate and specific information about the deceased loved ones (termed discarnates) of living people (termed sitters) even without any prior knowledge about the sitters or the discarnates and in the complete absence of any sensory sitter feedback. Moreover, the information reported by these mediums cannot be explained as a result of fraud or 'cold reading' (a set of techniques in which visual and auditory cues from the sitter are used to fabricate 'accurate' readings) on the part of the mediums or rater bias on the part of the sitters."

This brings us to the present. I'd say it's about time for us to connect the dots. We will do so in the next chapter.

Chapter Twelve
A New World View

We live in a world of information overload. So much comes at us every day it's impossible to take it all in. This may be one reason the water building up behind the dam has not yet broken through. Maybe so much information has numbed our minds, or put us all to sleep.

Nevertheless, the time has come to acknowledge we are not comparable to machines—as the nineteenth-twentieth century paradigm still holding sway would have us believe. We are not assemblies of parts that somehow evolved out of the muck and developed a computer-like organ called the brain that miraculously creates awareness inside our skulls. When the brain dies, the lights do not go out. We simply leave the old worn out vehicle behind and go on to other things.

The lights do not go out because the brain and the body are simply means to an end. The brain-body combination is a way for spirit—the life force, a spark of the godhead—to enter into physical reality. Perhaps we come here one time. Perhaps we come here hundreds or even thousands of times. Perhaps physical reality is like a great big amusement park—a diversion. Perhaps it is a school. I think it's both, and we come here to learn. What are we here to learn? Many things. But compassion may top the list. In the spirit realm, there are no starving people. There is no need to come up with rent money. There is no physical pain.

Whatever the reason or reasons we come here, the physical realm is not our home. Spirit is our home.

This time in history is the right time for us to realize who we are and what we are doing here because many of us have lost our way. We've forgotten who we are. We are eternal. We are constantly evolving. We are sparks of the Divine. Getting more material stuff we will someday have to leave behind will not help us grow.

A New World View

In the past, a single discovery could create a new world view—that the earth was round, or that the sun was the center of the solar system. Then Newton's laws followed by the *Origin of Species* did the trick. It seems to me so many discoveries have occurred since then that more than enough are on the table to create a new one.

What's holding us back? Those with a vested interest in maintaining the status quo. People who do not want to look stupid. Ignorance on the part of people too caught up in the information overload to see the forest for the trees. People with dogmatic religious beliefs. The truth is, a new world view is already held in part by many, and in full by a small percentage of the population in the West today.

Ironically, the new world view is not fundamentally different from that which existed before self awareness caused humans to feel separated from the rest of nature. It is that mind—the intelligent medium of thought postulated by Thomas Troward—is the ground of being of all that is, and that we and everything in the universe are not only connected to it and to each other, we are each aspects of it. We are at one with nature, part of one mind. In our new understanding that the Divine animates us all, we have come full circle, yet we have arrived on higher ground in terms of our depth of our understanding.

Aspects and Implications of the New World View

The new world view—that we are aspects of one mind—has a number of implications. It can accommodate both science and religion and bring the two together—although each will need to make adjustments to eliminate what will now be seen as aberrant dogma.

Both Thomas Troward and Scott Peck were correct. The ground of being is the life force, the medium of thought, that pushes in the direction of growth and evolution—producing the phenomenon Peck called grace. The realization it exists solves the problem inherent in Darwin's theory of evolution—the lack of a counterbalance to the Law of Entropy.

Rupert Sheldrake is right. Sub fields exist within this field. Lovelock was correct—the earth, Gaia, has a field. Each species has a field. Each person has a field we call a soul. Sub fields are individual and yet at one with the whole just as television transmissions represent a single bandwidth and separate channels simultaneously.

The life force, Tao, or God does not play favorites. As Jesus said, "[God] causes his sun to rise on the evil and the good and sends rain on the righteous and unrighteous." (Matthew 5:45)

The field of mind supports and fosters life and harmony of body, mind and spirit. Prayer—some prefer the word "intention"—can add energy to this. Studies that show more and higher-quality prayer or intention will bring greater results.

How to Make Life Work and Purposeful

Because our minds are objective, we have the power of choice or "free will." This gives us the ability to attune our thoughts and actions with the direction of the life force—toward growth, evolution, and harmony. It gives us the power to recognize the compassionate self within. It gives us the power to go within and commune with the Universal Mind, the Tao, or the Holy Spirit—whatever name you may wish to give the ground of being within.

By aligning ourselves and subjugating our wills to the Universal Mind, we "go with the flow" and life works better for us. When we push against the force and try to counteract or contain it, we experience difficulties. I go into detail about this in my book, *THE TRUTH*.

Syncronicities Are Real

The universal mind matches things up that may benefit from being matched up—called synchronicity—in its push toward growth and evolution. Life, health and harmony within an organism are supported perforce. In all matters, the outcome that will produce the maximum amount of evolution receives top priority. The Universal Mind will make events work in such a way that even the most horrible tragedy will produce the maximum good possible. This may be the meaning behind the Apostle Paul's words in Romans 8:28, "And we know that in all things God works for the good of those who love him." That they love him means they are striving to evolve in order to become more like him.

Let's face it, difficulties often force us to evolve and to become better people as a result.

Our Views and Attitudes Create Our Experiences

God is within us. Therefore, the personality of the God our objective mind assumes exists will be the personality of the God we come to know because the subjective mind within plays back what we impress upon it. If we assume a loving and forgiving father God, as Jesus said to do, this will be our God. If someone assumes a loving mother God, instead, this will be that person's experience.

If one believes in an unforgiving, wrathful and capricious God, this will be the God that person has to deal with.

If a person does not believe in God at all, but thinks everything happens arbitrarily and by chance, this will be that person's experience.

If a person believes that God will punish him for his transgressions, that person will be punished. Outside circumstances combined with beliefs become a person's reality. To change your reality, change your beliefs.

The same is true in matters of health. If a person believes the body is subject to all sorts of influences beyond his control, and that this, that, or another symptom shows that such and such an uncontrollable influence is at work on him, then the belief will impress itself on the subjective mind, the subjective mind will accept it without question and proceed to fashion bodily conditions in accordance with the belief. Once someone fully grasps this, he or she will see it is just as easy to externalize healthy conditions as it is the contrary.

You Are Eternal, We All Are Eternal

What else?

Your current incarnation may be one of a long line than dates to the first life on earth, or some other planet. Your physical body is a projection of your morphogenetic field in combination with those of your parents, their genes, and the morphogenetic field of the species. In this lifetime you are a composite of your soul, which is eternal and essentially unchanging, the genes and morphogenetic field of the family you were born into, and the environment in which you grew up. The you of this life will eventually be incorporated into your soul as you evolve throughout eternity.

When we die, our souls return to spirit—the mental realm. We may be members of a group who work together. We may be guides to one another. We may incarnate together often—as part of a group of souls that cooperate to help one another advance.

All creation is one connected whole, with no separate pieces. We are the whole, and the whole is us. What happens here influences what happens there, even if it is halfway across the galaxy. Energy takes time to travel, but information is transmitted instantaneously because only one mind exists.

Cultivate Your Garden

Although I don't think it's always the case, each lifetime on Earth usually has a particular purpose. It may be to learn a lesson. It may be to help others in some way. Some have missions they agreed to before an incarnation. When this is the case, the circumstances of one's life support the accomplishment of that mission.

In my opinion, there is no greater joy in life than doing what you are here to do. Getting to that point may be difficult, but a person will get there if he or she listens and perseveres. Eventually, grace will kick in. After a while, a person following an innate calling will begin to sense unseen guiding hands, and the way will become less difficult. The trials won't be as hard to bear. There will be blind alleys, of course. There will be disappointments. There will be tough lessons to learn, but gradually that person will come to a gut level understanding of what his or her existence as a human being is about and the purpose of this particular life on earth. That person will come to know what he or she is doing and see outcomes materializing before the destination is reached.

When a person arrives at this point, that person will realize he or she has come to power, spiritual power, and with this realization will come joy. Imagine the buoyant feeling. Whether it's mastery of a sport such as golf or tennis, mastery of the card game of bridge, a musical instrument or a foreign language, the arrival at the state of really knowing what you are doing always brings joy.

Now that you have grasped the new world view, that's what I wish for you. Mastery at what you came here to do. It makes sense to pursue it, don't you agree?

May the riches of the universe—which are in fact non material—flow effortlessly to you because you are working with the universe, rather than rowing against the tide.

About the Author

Stephen Hawley Martin spent the first twenty-five years of his adult life in the advertising business. He enjoyed the people and the work, but decided it was time to move on in order to pursue a lifelong desire to find out and share the truth about life. He is now the author or editor of more than a dozen books and has won half a dozen national book awards for excellence.

Stephen Hawley Martin

If you would like to hear the radio interviews he references in this book, go to his web site, SHMartin.com, look to the top left of the home page, and click on "Science of LAD Interviews."